HUNGER ENOUGH

Living Spiritually in a Consumer Society

Edited by Nita Penfold, D.Min.

HUNGER ENOUGH $18

Living Spiritually in a Consumer Society

Edited by Nita Penfold, D.Min.

Pudding House Publications
ISBN 1-58998-249-5

Copyright © 2004 Pudding House Publications
All rights reserved.
Copyright for individual work remains with authors;
Pudding House retains permission to reprint.
To copy any of these poems individually, permission
must first be obtained from the author in writing,
citing at least the full title of this book and the publisher.
FIRST EDITION
Printed in the United States of America

Editor: Nita Penfold
Publisher & Managing Editor: Jennifer Bosveld
Publications Director: Bob Worrall
Editorial team: Jim Bosveld, Doug Swisher, Steve Abbott, Kathleen Burgess

Pudding House Publications
81 Shadymere Lane
Columbus Ohio 43213
614-986-1881
info@puddinghouse.com www.puddinghouse.com

Cover *Mono Zero* copyright © 2004 Daniel Dancer.
ABOUT THE COVER: A *zerocircle* is a circular form built from found materials and left upon the land to function as Earth healing "medicine;" a hand-made expression of hope; a symbol of our trust in the Mystery. Each is a way of putting prayer into form. Every zerocircle helps ground our anger over what is happening to the ecosystems which sustain us. Every zerocircle marks a personal commitment to fight for wild nature and help end the destruction of our public lands. Photo taken in Chequamegon National Forest, Wisconsin. From www.inconcertwithnature.com, daniel@inconcertwithnature.com.

Opinions expressed in these poems are the views of the authors
and do not necessarily reflect the views of the editors.

All Pudding House Publications are archived by The Ohio State University Libraries Special Collections, SUNY/Buffalo Lockwood Library Special Collections, Kent State University Library Special Collections, Brown University Library, Poets House/NYC, a few private collectors, and the Library at Pudding House Innovative Writers Programs. Books are listed in Bowker/*Books in Print* and may be ordered through Pudding House at www.puddinghouse.com. Pudding House extends generous discounts to independent bookstores, non-profit organizations, writers' groups, and special events.

ACKNOWLEDGMENTS

Gratitude is expressed to the editors of the following publications
in which these poems appeared:

Antler: "Hearing the Echo," *Selected Poems*; "Star-Struck Utopias of
the 21st Century," *Poems*
Miriam Axel-Lute: "Souls Like Mockingbirds," *Souls Like
Mockingbirds*
Miriam Ben-Yaacov: "Ways to World Peace," *Prairie Wind*
Richard Alan Bunch: "Voyages," *Neovictorian/Cochlea*
Anne Coray: "Directions," first appeared in *Albatross* and was reprinted
in *Ivory;* "Becoming the Moon," *Ivory*
Stephen Corey: "The Tempest," *All These Lands You Call One Country*
Barbara Crooker: "Barbie and Ken Maximize Their Options," *Nebraska
Territory*; "From the Museum of Natural History,"*Laughing
Unicorn*
Daniel Dancer: "Breaking the Spell," *Shards and Circles: Artistic
Adventures in Spirit and Ecology*
Karen Ethelsdattar: "Making Play," *Mothering Magazine*
Mary Krane Derr: "Why Should I Care," *Free Press Green Pages*
Charles Kesler: "What's Next?" *Krax*
David Kowalczyk: "Logic of Conspicuous Consumption," *Oyez Review*
Mary Laufer: "At The Top of the Food Chain," *Pemmican;* "Our
Conscience," *Out of Line*
Gabrielle LeMay: "Nativity," *Medical Purposes Literary Review*
Ellen Lindquist: "How the Pitiless Sprinkler Ushered in the
Apocalypse," *Flashshot Daily Genre Flash Fiction*
Lou Lipsitz: "Watching the TV Version of the Holocaust," *Kansas
Quarterly*
Robert Aquinas McNally: "Their Gathering," *Hawaii Pacific Review*
Julia Older: "Valiant Soldiers," *We Speak For Peace*
Lee Patton: "Dismantling Hell at the Old Dump," *College of the
Redwoods Del Norte*
Nita Penfold: "Discipline," *The Buffalo News*
Dalene Stull: "Seeds," *Best of Ohio, 2000*

Dedicated to
Rev. Jim Bosveld

HUNGER ENOUGH
Living Spiritually in a Consumer Society
Edited by Nita Penfold, D.Min.

Contents

II. Breaking the Spell

Foreword

Because I wanted help living spiritually
in this consumer society

During the early development of Rev. Jim Bosveld's road to ministry, major elements of his learning combined with his lifelong studies in history, justice work, and law to create a panoramic vision of how serious attention to true Peace and social justice addresses deep ecology as well. Social justice and environmental concerns are tightly linked; therefore, it seems to me we should have an easier time enticing all of us toward healthier decisions.

With this in mind, Jim developed an 8-session lecture series that educated participants about consumer realities and some healing alternatives. He invited experts to speak on various subjects from organic farming to the media monopoly (see Rev. Bosveld's Afterword) and invited the public to an open forum after the lectures. The series was first offered at the UU Congregation East/Columbus and by the Wayne County UU Church/Wooster. These events were open to the public—a gift to communities.

I learned from Jim that attention for community-supported pro-environmental choices would result in equally wise decisions for social programming that empowers the poor and could change the cycle of poverty. It is all connected.

The American popular culture is gluttonous, and this disposable lifestyle of super-want has a huge negative impact on what we're willing to do for the poor, whether there is a sustainable inventory of resources, and whether the poor are given meaningful opportunities to "bring themselves up by their bootstraps" as many of us like to expect. It also has an impact on our health, our supplies for tomorrow, whether or not we're getting the news. Where's the water that is safe to bathe in, much less drink? While some of us are trying to assure that what we ingest is safe enough, many of us are wanting it also to be perfect. We are paradoxical creatures. While I eat at many fine restaurants, I run a nearly empty refrigerator and know the high of using the last piece of bread in the loaf, the last scrape from the jam jar. Shoshauna Shy's "The Suggestion of Slivers" speaks for me, "...weekly/ I let the refrigerator empty/ and watch my children forage..."

If we think change is needed by the poor themselves (better life skills, less "acting out"), it is even more all consumers who can change everything.   Consumption, collecting outrageous numbers of things, "having," is the major addiction in this country.   Manufacture and distribution with little conscience combines with that addiction to create a toxic life-style for everyone on Earth.   What I call "Buy it and Bury it." We're putting more and more at the curb and into the landfill.

I've been seeking a deeper understanding of that Interdependent Web of Life that would demand both social justice motives and environmental advocacy that results in mutual blessings.   Some of my buying practices have changed as a result of the slightest education: from the poets, from reputable independent publications, from my husband over the years, and as I attended a few of the Living Spiritually in a Consumer Society (LSCS) presentations.   I choose some organic options now (when it's convenient, I confess) where I never did before, and I'm a publisher using more recycled paper and soy inks.   I'm not bragging.   I look to be increasingly conscious about my choices.   That is why I wanted Pudding House to publish a collection of poems on consumption, examining how we might live more spiritually in this society that seems to express itself out from and back into a cycle of buy and dispose—a consumption-based economy.

The perception is that we must keep making more in order to sell more, in order to keep people employed, so they can buy more and be happy and keep companies operating and keep people employed, etc.   Is this a cycle we want to break?   If so, why?   Is anyone successful at living another way, let alone a whole community of people?   We need help seeing the problems in the first place then finding alternatives, understanding the psychological and sociological issues, changing our opinions on the difference between what we "need" and what we "want."

The point is to have *hunger enough* to survive (even comfortably and joyously) without hungering for far more than our share.   This is a tough thing to convince anyone of.   Poetry convinces me when other forms of expression fail.   So we've called in the poets.

Rev. Bosveld's series on intentional living is the inspiration for this project and for the new web-based *Intentional Living Journal* at www.puddinghouse.com.   Jim and I asked Nita Penfold to direct the editorial work and call for poems, to select, and to organize this book.   Her work pleases us greatly.

These poems represent a dynamic range of subject matter, a wide selection of relevant consumer activity, and there are many well-crafted poems of artistic merit.   The collection is hard-hitting, but I don't think it will tire the reader.   It isn't designed to make us feel guilty and repent, but rather to feel like we're not alone in the struggle and that there is hope.

Nita Penfold holds a Doctorate in Ministry from Matthew Fox's University of Creation Spirituality.   She works as the Director of Religious

Education at the First Parish in Lexington (Unitarian-Universalist), Massachusetts, and as an artist in residence and adjunct faculty at Andover Newton Theological School. She is a widely published poet whose work has appeared in anthologies: *Woman Prayers* (HarperSanFrancisco), *Cries of the Spirit* (Beacon Press), *Claiming the Spirit Within* (Beacon Press), *If I Had My Life to Live Over I Would Pick More Daisies* (Papier Mache Press) and *Catholic Girls* (Plume/Penguin), among others. Two chapbooks of her work have been published by our press: *The Woman With the Wild-Grown Hair* and *Mile-High Blue-Sky Pie*. I thank Nita for the energy she gave this good work and for her passion for poetry and a quality human experience on Earth.

—Jennifer Bosveld, Publisher and Managing Editor

Introduction

"The soul of the world makes its revelations felt not by lecturing us that there is something wrong with our endless wanting, but by giving us glimpses of a numinous experience of life that stops our wanting in its tracks, because in that state we simply do not require anything else to complete ourselves, except, perhaps, the one continuing desire of all desires, to bring that vital celebration of experience into the center of our existence."
—David Whyte, *The Heart Aroused*

A few years ago I was discussing my doctoral work at the University of Creation Spirituality with a man clearly in deep despair at the laundry list of seemingly unsolvable issues that spelled disaster for the planet. This included the depletion of the ozone, massive pollution of the atmosphere, the water, and the soil in our pursuit of resources and industrial advancements, planned obsolescence and the attitude that we can just throw everything somewhere else to get rid of it (usually in poor people's backyards), the proliferation of violence, and the great disparity between rich and poor. He asked me how I could go on day by day with this, how I could have any kind of hope in this situation. We were destroying the planet, and he worried for the future of his daughter and other children.

I told him that I felt Earth tries to compensate for our recklessness but will eventually destroy the parasites that are consuming more than their share of resources. The earth will survive and heal itself, but human beings will have essentially destroyed themselves. We as a species have, by some accounts, only a small window of opportunity—50 years or so— to turn around our destruction. And that I am part of the problem. The only thing that I can do is to change myself, examine my attitudes and become aware of what I am really hungering for, struggle with my choices and make better ones. And I can hope that others will do the same by talking about it, sharing resources, and teaching the children.

The man seemed a little stunned by what I said, but came back a few weeks later to tell me that our conversation had made him feel less despair. Everyone else he had talked to had denied that the problem was that large, or else despaired that there was nothing that could be done. By naming our destruction out like that, he was affirmed in his thoughts—he wasn't going crazy, there was a big problem, and he had to do what he could do in his own life to alter it. It might work or it might not, but he could also choose to have hope.

In essence, that is what this book is about. It is about naming our despair and making our choices. It is about becoming aware of what impact our lives are having on this planet of which we are a part but not masters. It is about not getting caught in the quagmire of despair where one cannot move, but about choosing to have hope that we can still make a difference in our own lives. It is an awesome responsibility. We have lost our place in the scheme of things. We need to recognize that the hunger that human beings have to make meaning of their lives, to connect with some greater purpose, has gotten short circuited into a hunger to own *things*, and that hunger has consumed us because it can never be fully satisfied with *things*. What we hunger for is so much greater than a new CD or the latest fashion; we hunger to find the way back to ourselves and our place as an interdependent part of this wonderful living system called Earth.

In choosing the work for this book, I concentrated on those who took responsibility for what is happening, who struggle with the hungering for enough, who question their choices and keep trying to live a centered life where the core of their living is not based on consumerism. I winnowed the many wonderful poems and prose pieces down to two sections, those that I felt touched each part of the human psyche and human weakness and those that could give some sense of hope and reached out to a greater meaning and greater connection to something much larger than themselves. I chose work from people who put themselves in the middle of the equation using the words "I" and "we" instead of "they," who accepted their culpability in this culture and tried to name and change it by taking that first step to change—awareness. There are no definitive solutions here for the 21st Century plight in this society of rampant consumerism, resource depletion, and managed degradation of the human soul. But there is a sense of humor at ourselves and our weaknesses and a sense of hope about what we can accomplish when we slow down and remember to breathe.

Matthew Fox, theologian and teacher, has written: "Whether our species is sustainable or not depends on our wrestling creativity back from the brink of its demonic potential." (*Creativity: Where the Divine and Human Meet*) I offer this anthology as one place where there is that hope.

—Nita Penfold, D.Min., Editor

I. The Price We Pay

The Naming Of Things

We name the world to console ourselves.
Hands point to the numbers on a clock.
Sipping tea from a cup, we place lip upon lip
and drink rose hips, fleshy center of the flower.

The bulbous legs of a table remind me of a relative
from the old country. They sink down
into the flowery crimson carpet, unbudging
and thick with dignity.

The metal teeth of a saw bite into limbs
to spit out chips of pine and oak.
The teeth of a comb can find white lice that love
the delicate hairs at the nape of the neck.

Through the mouth of a cave, through limestone
built of tiny sea bodies, we enter the earth.
Veins of ore run through rock, variegated
layers of lodestone and gold.

In the puckered navel of an orange the unborn fruit
is tucked. A beetle crawls along the leathery neck
of a squash. Eyes look back at us from the leaf bud
of a potato, from the still small center of a cyclone—

no rain in sight. We walk on bound soles
in transitory bodies. Spines of leatherbound books
list the ways of longing, spell out our loneliness
in the nominal world.

Jan Lee Ande

Nativity

Where stars have crashed down and the earth is torn,
Adam paces Eden's steamy mud:
A woman shrieks and a baby is born.

The baby has babies, builds a hut, plants corn,
beans, peas, and wheat—and blesses every bud
where stars have crashed down and the earth is torn.

Now Adam blesses paychecks. Toxic toys adorn
his plastic homestead; Eden is awash in industrial crud.
A woman shrieks and a baby is born

into spiritual poverty: boredom, scorn,
and hopelessness engulf him in a caustic flood
where stars have crashed down and the earth is torn.

And now we are possessed of a malignant thorn
that has poisoned our semen and our torpid blood;
a woman shrieks and a baby is born

to wink out and die. There's little time to mourn.
Coffin after coffin makes a shuddering thud
where stars have crashed down and the earth is torn.
A woman shrieks and a baby is born…

Gabrielle LeMay

Barbie and Ken Maximize Their Options,

have a Jacuzzi and a Jenn-Aire in their condo,
time-share their vacations, drive a Porsche
and a Jeep. Buy extra-virgin olive oil,
wear natural fibers, faux furs.
Only eat organically grown fruit,
free-ranging chickens, oat bran pizza,
drink dry beer. Barbie works in an industrial
park; Ken's in military intelligence.
When wintering in tropical
paradise, they use sunscreens with SPFs of 30+.
Don't use aerosol sprays. Floss religiously.
Barbie and Ken eat chilled steamed jumbo shrimp
on their air-conditioned patio. See Barbie at the pool,
stretching out her long, long legs, her ever-pointed toes.
See Ken smile his blinding white smile. Look at his hair:
it never needs mousse or gel or conditioning creme.
Why, they are perfect, forever young,
no laugh lines, crow's feet, fallen arches;
eternally non-biodegradable.

Barbara Crooker

Price Club

They all lead here: Expressways, interstates and parkways
to the warehouse, members only, where yellow, orange and red
        shopping carts
wheel possible purchase. A young girl's eyes roll up in sleep as
        she dreams of magic markers

and glossy picture books. What voice commands, *Come on
        down*? My wallet, *Go ahead.*
I look up to barbecues and vacuum cleaners on raised altars,
huge cereal boxes like Warhol designs, paper plates stacked
        like southern columns.

My feet fast-forward on concrete: Do I want, do I want? I am
Solomon between expense and uselessness; in my basket, a new
        purse, pitas, cat food,
eager to be taken elsewhere, like me. I want

transubstantiation, to be taken up in corn flakes, Liz Claiborne
        and Fancy Feast.
If I choose wisely, a bell will ring, the cashier will wish me a
        nice day,
and I will preside over a new estate, closing cupboards

safely over bright-labeled cans, arranging lipstick and comb in
        my new purse,
that yields them back as I need them, my small fiefdom,
the serfs I can count on, their tactile faces loyal and willing.

Ann Cefola

In Consideration of Things

There are possessions that live longer
Than animals or humans,
Alien to everything around them.
Their purposes long forgotten,

They live out their days under my roof,
Unwelcome as squatters who pay nothing
While filling up all unused spaces.
They must have called out

To someone else
Who lived in my body once—
Called out to someone
Who loves the very

Things I despise—
(Which now litter each and every room),
Someone who hates all I
So dearly love.

When a deathly fatigue takes me under,
In a kind of near drowning,
I find that I must swim for my life
In the wake of hideous excess.

In my remade childhood,
My mother remains the librarian she always was,
Her books and call numbers giving order
To the chaotic world, her hands flying with purpose.

My father takes a different job—
At the busy corner hardware store.
They save the world, my parents:
She with her books and he with his religion,

Repair having become his sacred creed.
In the land of screws and washers,

He is a Holy Man who returns hungry each day at dusk,
Bearing light bulbs and small pieces of hardware.

Everything in our home—everything we own works,
And he!—he has lost his need for liquor while I
Want nothing more than the books Mother carries
Home in her small, grateful hands.

Mary Junge

I Become a Political Traitor

Shopping list, coupons, and unbleached canvas bags in hand
I firmly grasp a cart with no wobbly wheels
and stride across the parking lot.
I am unstoppable, I am a woman with a goal:
veggies, meat, milk, cereal, coffee, eggs, fruit—
everything on my list in thirty minutes or less.

I enter the store and am confronted with
a looming tower of fragrant, luscious, ripe, red,
perfectly unblemished strawberries
the saliva fountains up, but I have to ask
"Are they union picked?"
The produce guy ignores me.

Around the corner is the lettuce—
"Are these union too?"
He rolls his eyes,
"Jeez lady, I'm union. Don't that make a difference?"
"Yeah, your boss gives you a bathroom to use."
Even my thoughts are small.

I skip the apples.
According to the latest list that
Greenpeace shoved under my door,
if I want to avoid toxins
I'm supposed to eat thick skinned fruit,
except I remember that documentary
where Dole Corporation was starving
Indonesian farmers off their ancestral land
so I pick through the yellow landslide
searching fruitlessly for a bunch of bananas without
DOLE stickered on them.

Suddenly my willpower melts
under the sweet torture of the strawberries
and I stuff a pint in the corner of my cart.
Next on my list is meat
so I get some mysterious chicken parts wrapped in oozing
          plastic
decorated with cartoons of happy, fat chickens
and try not to think about flyers PETA shoved under my door—
drugs, disease, factory farming, slaughterhouses.

The cereal aisle looms bright and beckoning.
Okay, what was it—Nestle, bad. General Mills, good.
Or was it the other way around?
Damn I don't remember which one I'm supposed to boycott.
Oatmeal, now there's a compromise—
hopefully there's not too many pesticides in this,
hopefully not too many small farms went under
to large scale oat-farming agribusiness,
hopefully my karma won't
make me come back as a cockroach.

Coffee, coffee, must have my caffeine!
Wait! I don't want my $3.59 spent on a cash crop export
to collapse an entire third world economic system.

Then again I don't want to have a headache every day this
week.

I complete my mission with
a quart of milk from a BGH inflated cow
and a dozen brown eggs
fresh from the battery farm where
they put the chickens under lights 24 hours a day
until they lay themselves to death
and then grind the dead bodies to feed the rest.

Standing in line waiting for
the sullen clerk to ring my order
I scavenge the bottom of my bag
for every last coin and pray—

Forgive me insect,
forgive me chicken,
forgive me cow,
forgive me farmworker,
forgive me small farmer,
forgive me trees,
forgive me plants,
forgive me water,
forgive me world,
forgive me for being too poor
to buy my food in the health food store.

Sara Littlecrow-Russell

Development

Standing in my red pines I watched what seemed
to be a giant, orange insect feeding in the ditch
up and down the gravel road, tended by slaves
who served it chain-sawed plum, willow, cherry,
maple, tangled rolls of multiflora rose.

What it didn't consume they burned. Stacked
trunks cracked and popped, white plumes rose,
followed by red flames, and at last oily smoke
that swept across the sky like locusts. Ash
settled in my hair as I watched the crew

bulldoze stumps and boulders, shovel sawdust,
then huddle like weary soldiers, smoking until
their boss and the Road Commissioner arrived
in a spotless Dodge pickup. Out they leaped,
all business, with clipboard and blueprints.

I knew the developer's vision, what he and his
computer dreamed: roadsides groomed like
golf-course greens, four lanes of polished
pavement to speed buyers to five-acre plots
in another pretend natural paradise.

Soon surveyors were planting red-flagged poles
in the pasture, measuring the woods, spraying
white "X's" on tree trunks. I heard graders and
chainsaws, trucks advancing through the gears.
Smelled diesel fumes. The earth shook.

One night in my sleep two speeding lights forced
fox, rabbits, possums, groundhogs, skunk, deer,
squirrels, coons into a shredder's spinning steel
blades. Covering my ears, I looked up; waves
of birds fled into the moon. It closed.

When I awoke towering lamps outshone sunrise,
motors droned, horns honked, houses blocked

the skyline, birds sang from metal speakers.
Instead of pines people stood staring at my
cabin. Insects crawled from their eyes.

Edward Beatty

Dominion

A hundred acres of moneywood
no god-damned forester ever marked
and you're whining about warblers?
This is end time.
Cut those trees or somebody else will.

We'll come with Satan's own machines
our John Deere $50,000 fellerbunchers-skidders-chippers*,
and work 'em to death.
We'll twitch those logs and skid 'em,
leave nothin' but stumps, air
and empty bottles of Allen's coffee-flavored brandy.

$480 per 12-cord load trucked to the mill
and 18-wheelers full of chips.
They get their toilet paper,
we pay John Deere,
you get cash and acres of free rolling
clearcut with memories
of bears feeding on the beechnuts.

Jacqueline Moore

*Machines used in heavy impact forestry.

Palm Lines

They come in bulldozers
on weekends when the officials
who have not been bought off
are less likely to appear.

The mangroves go first,
cleared
for piers
for the large boats favored
by the rich who will prove to be
good stewards of the land,
once the land has been reshaped
in their images.

The fill comes fast:
Dump truck dump truck dump truck dump truck,
incoming passing outgoing passing
incoming:
Bulldozers arrange the loads like children
in a sandbox, pushing and piling
within the box.

Now the land is right.
Now the land is ready.
Now the land, now covered over, is as it has always been. Who
among us can say otherwise?

The land now filled, the mangroves now as
gone as next year's water birds. The permits
now applied for
and got
from county employees
whose palms are now greener
than yesterday's wetlands.

Richard Downing

Dismantling Hell at the Old Dump

We swerve toward the sea bluffs
laughing about when this park was the dump
and we'd be stashed in back of Dad's pickup—
itself a candidate for the scrap-heap—
hunkered among the week's trash
as if we ourselves were candidates
for expulsion over those slimy,
guano-topped rocks.

Tidied by the hands of wary heirs,
the beach of broken glass, of beer-
bottle ambers and sea-greens, rough edges
soothed by twenty thousand tides,
has smoothed into local attraction,
"Glass Beach," where tourists
rove barefoot over a crush of shards—
our parents' and grandparents' discards
too worthless for the penny deposit.

As if in crusty mockery,
twisted, rusted almost through,
stubborn fingers of scrap metal
stretch like old men's palsied claws
from the tops of sea rocks. Fat seals
doze on the lower ledges. Today,
locals yammer about the seals
"taking over"—transmitted on the AM
feeding-frenzy of fact-free disdain, callers
equate "environmental law" with Satan.

But Hell was actually dismantled here
when the eternal trash fires were doused
among smoldering rags and cat carcasses
jumbled down bluffs to trash tides
of shoe-polish tins and condoms, seasoned
by a fresh stream of raw sewage, puked
airborne into the Pacific like talk-radio spew,

the shuck of unpolished families
who didn't know from Shinola
about not defiling our own home.

Lee Patton

Hollow Hearts

Just as his father did, Virgil farms two hundred acres
and mid-summer baptizes his potatoes with poisons
disguised as superheroes—like Tordon or Eptam,
sons of the chemical giants of Cenex and Monsanto.

Virgil bends down slowly over all the earth
as though he's the giver of life, and returns
holding a spud caked with dirt, brown—a baker.
He slices the flesh with his pocket knife. The fruit
is full and firm. No hollow hearts here he determines
pushing the cap back on his brow like a runner
who just stole home.

He watches the pivots spew water over
soil turned on itself, moisten the velvet
loam plied with perfumed toxins.
He scrawls numbers in his notepad, licks
his lips. He knows full well the bargain
he makes, and with whom. Throwing
his shovel in the back he drives his pickup
home, taking the long way around
his hollow heart.

Ellen Waterston

The Abundant Cow

Grows rooted in its box of shit
like broccoli, cross-bred for meat
and placidity until the reflection in
its eyes of wonder and adventure is
almost gone, like the ghost of a distant
pine tree vaguely seen through heavy snow.

Tim Amsden

This Just In...

At nine a.m. this morning in an unnamed South American republic, six thousand cows were reported married to anonymous mates in a mass ceremony led by Reverend Sun Moon Moo, alias Mr. MooMacker, charismatic mogul of multinational fast feed chain, MOOMACKERS.

The cows were reportedly happily orbiting the earth this afternoon in what's alleged to be the world's first mass bovine honeymoon.

Recently Reverend Moo has come under attack by both environmental groups and health advocates for contributing to the decline of world health by serving burgers so heavily laced with estrogen that they grow breasts and for the virtual obliteration of the globe's oxygen producing rainforests. When asked to respond to the groups the Reverend had this to say, "Let them eat beef."

When questioned further about widespread accusations of heavy investment in the now booming door-to-door oxygen delivery industry, Reverend Moo stalwartly denied, admitting later, when pressed, to having installed 4,322 coin-operated oxygen machines in MOOMACKERS Restaurants this month, claiming, "Those things bring in less than juke boxes and erotic video games combined."

In response to complaints from gagging customers, Reverend Moo has pledged to divert one tenth of one percent of net profits to a special fund that would not only launch the remaining eighteen acres of tropical rain forest on a world tour, but would also assure a free potted palm with every burger sold.

Tamra Plotnick

How the Pitiless Sprinkler Ushered in the Apocalypse

As the sprinkler's power swelled, it leveled the prefabricated house where a pond had once been. The sprinkler felt for the former body of water drained for the sake of erecting an aluminum frame. Then it turned its wrath upon the filling station. Gas drained into sewers, houses burst into flame and the unforgiving sprinkler refused to put the fires out.

Ellen Lindquist

Is That Chicken Organic?

Excuse me...sir...
Is that chicken organic?
That one, there
When that chicken was still kickin'
was she fed wholesome, all-organic meal
free of treacherous hormones and antibiotics?
Did she get to roam the range
foraging and frolicking through amber waves of organic grain?

During her stay at *Rancho de Pollo*
was this hen provided with a firm futon
private phone, yoga classes and
her pick of the roosters?
Was she sexually fulfilled?
Did she lay Jumbo brown happy eggs like it says on the carton?
I mean, can you certify that this bird
right here led a full and rich life
up until the day some thoughtful soul
whacked off her head
bled her dry and plucked her naked?
Did she grow up in a nurturing, incest-free family
with a multi-cultural education and her own web site
before she was skinned, shrink-wrapped and shipped to market?
Did my little child of god have access to the panoply of 12-step
        programs
for any recovery issues that might arise for one who was
born to be broiled?
Please assure me that she went through life without
suffering irradiation or genetically engineered anything

See, my body is sooooo sensitive
I've got to make sure that whatever I consume meets
the highest standards of purity and nutritional excellence
If I am what I eat and I'm gonna eat meat
I mean second-hand grains: predigested, bio-converted grub
well, then my conversion machine—my chicken—
had better be fueled by organic grains that were
hand-harvested under a full moon by vine-ripened virgins

Yes, I need to know all the details of my happy hen's diet and
lifestyle choices
Was her aura cleansed of negative psychic energies
before I sautéed her in cold-pressed flax seed oil
with a hint of fresh rosemary?
Was a spiritual advisor of her choosing present
during her final hours?
Were last rites administered while Susan Sarandon held
a candlelight prayer vigil outside the slaughterhouse?
Before I speared her tender flesh with the tines of my fork
before my teeth cut into her succulent thigh
for god's sake tell me she was treated humanely!
I care about these things

I may not be a vegetarian
but my chicken damn well better be

Lisa Martinović

What's Next?

I wonder what the next
I-gotta-get-me-one-of-
these-things is coming
out of the consumer chute
buckin' and snortin' and
kickin' until I ride
it peacefully into my credit
card quicksand convinced
I can't live without this
doodad. Do Dad tell me
how you got along without
a computer and internet
and whatever other net
the all-consuming God wants
to throw on me. Yes, God
is an all-consuming fire
and what they tell me
I really need is Reverend
H.O. Hornblower's $199
cassette tape series on "Living
Prosperously—Your Right
As A Child Of God." $399 on
video. If you order the
video series you get a bonus
video of Reverend Hornblower's
Christmas message "In All Your
Giving Make Sure God Gets His."
And of course I can charge it.
Operators are standing by.

Charles Kesler

Logic of Conspicuous Consumption

Robert DeNiro
eats
at Spago.

I
am eating
at Spago.

Therefore, I
must be
Robert DeNiro.

David Kowalczyk

Collector

In her home
there are no shrines,
no sage-scented sacred places
where acknowledged spirits linger
and the dead are fed
from candle flames.

She has only beautiful things,
whole clusters of beautiful things
with no center and no soul,
collections of beautiful things
that nudge and poke each other
feeling thirsty and claustrophobic.

Some go out for air
and search for a place
to form themselves into a shrine,
but they are only followed home
by even finer specimens
that throw themselves,
sacrificially, onto the piles
to be elbowed and kicked
by rare artifacts.

Who can live simply
among so much beauty?
Whole mounds of art
begin to mold and decompose
as if having been meant for food.
In dusty cupboards exquisite carvings
whisper among themselves,
plan their defection.
At night discontented treasures
begin knocking at the door
of her dreams. They want out.
Each asks to be alone
to be marveled at, praised,
surrounded by flowers,
to become a shrine
in the altar of her everyday.

Maureen Tolman Flannery

Toys

The Hindu concept of toys,
as Huston Smith describes it:

Let them race to the stores to buy
this season's bimbo dolls and superheroes
for glassy-eyed kids—

Let them add to their video libraries
the latest priceless collectors' editions—

Let them fill their houses with Southwestern bric-a-brac
in pastels utterly foreign to the mesa country—

Let them buy Land Rovers and Trans-Ams,
Lamborghinis and Lexus L-7's,
with 24-CD-changers in the trunks—
Let them amble from massage table to hot tub
to big-screen TV to Barca-Lounger to home pool table
to sauna—

Let them cut a dance tune with drum machine,
hit Number 1 and dominate the charts,
make a movie that bangs down eighty mil its opening
        weekend—

Let them purchase companies and corporations and
string them together like beads;
let them build their Aladdin's-cave portfolios—

Let them.
Someday, someday
(may it come in this life),
someday the sacred animal so deep within the self
will tire at last, will grow
hungry, will know true
hunger, will
long for
food.

Tim Myers

What I Thought Of At WalMart
(which I'm supposed to be boycotting)

I know I am supposed to be angry
about war and I should be marching, somewhere,
and I should be feeding the hungry and I should be
clicking on the "give a free mammogram" icon
on that website every day and I should
recycle more and not drink coffee
and I should now buy Mitsubishi and NOBODY
should eat veal although word of that seems
not to have gotten around to all the places it should
and somehow all of this makes me so very tired
and where would we even begin if we were so inclined
—and apparently we are—to fix this? Is anyone else exhausted
just thinking about this mess we've made, and is anyone
going to be offended if I say that sometimes
like tonight, as I'm driving out of the WalMart parking lot
under a hangnail of orange moon
with the success of supersize dogfood in the backseat
and a halfway decent song on the radio
I think that surely I would not trade this mess
for all the other neat and tidy lifetimes I could have chosen.

Annie Farnsworth

At The Top Of The Food Chain

Why should you care
that plankton is sensitive
to ultraviolet-B radiation?
How could tiny organisms that drift
in the ocean have anything to do with you?

What difference does it make
if embryos of long-toed salamanders
are being found with abnormal tails
and swollen bodies, or if deformed frogs
are turning up all over the country?

Do you still feel safe
when you hear that populations
of small animals are declining,
crabs and salmon and seabirds,
and no one is exactly sure why?

You can keep denying
that we are all connected
to each other, but deep down
you must know—
little things are the first to go.

Mary Laufer

Glut of Privilege

We are done with the sea.
With whale, shark and squid.
Done with the earth.
With elephant, skunk and snake.
Done as a roadside condom.

Dump them into a sack.
Dump the sack into a pit.
Dump the pit into the dark.
Dump the dark into the past.
Dump the past out of context.

This is not TV antennae on holy
temples. This is sealing our sequel
in the repeat we accumulate.
This is erasing our aftermath
with the profit we miscalculate.

Douglas Blazek

My Cellmate the Bear

Behind
your heavy eyes, I think
you are seeing green.

I think you see a heady forest, life
in every branch, earth
beneath
your mighty tread.

Now
there is not strength left
for you
to hate your cage.

I want to lead you
in a scream, a bellow—
to tell you that there is such a thing
as Beauty, and this world
is not only the bite of asphalt
and steep bars.

Soft Reverence
is just
sleeping.

But,
this strange fabric
hurts my skin.
It has been so long
since I saw
the moon.
Rhythms that should drum-dance
through my veins
from the ground the sky the river
forming rapture pumping life

have left me.

And I have lost the path
to any forest
I would hope to give you.

Aubrey Ryan

42

Confinement

Come in, come in. Yes, it is a bit crowded, I know. Some of you can stand outside. There in the hallway. The rest of you, have a seat. Well no, I don't really have any chairs. The carpet is quite comfortable, though.

So? What do you think? Simple, isn't it? I love simplicity. That's why I choose to live in my closet. Simplicity.

Oh yes, living here is quite voluntary. Quite voluntary. That house you walked through on your way here? Mine. Mine alone since my husband left. He was the last to go, you see. Long after the children we built the house for. My husband…he used to make all the decisions. For both of us.

Then he was gone. Leaving me with all the choices. Overwhelming! Think about what I had to decide. Every single day. To begin with, breakfast. A simple meal? Well you might think so. Especially when it's just cereal and tea. But…Ten kinds of cereal in the cupboard. Flakes or granola or biscuits? And my tea. Caffeinated or decaf or herbal? Which flavor? Oh, I was really dizzy by the time I had it ready.

Then, where to eat? The table on the little porch outside the back door? But maybe there would be bugs. The breakfast room table? But it seats eight—too big for just me. A tray in the family room while I watch TV? Every day those choices. I lost my appetite. Thought about just going back to bed. Sooner or later, though I had to get dressed.

Came in here with a sinking heart. This very closet. Can you imagine? I had so many clothes then…All this space wasn't even enough. True. Out-of-season clothes were in another bedroom closet. Too-small clothes, you know, the ones that might fit someday when the moon was in the right orbit? They were still in another closet.

Let's see, I'd think, what should I wear? I hear you. What's the big deal? Why not just jeans and a T-shirt? Okay, black or brown jeans? Dark blue, stone-washed, chartreuse, khaki? Even white jeans. My husband had my clothes arranged by color—light to dark. Dressy jeans, casual jeans? Bell-bottom, boot-cut, straight leg? Which one of fifty T-shirts or thirty belts? And shoes? Heaps of them. Jumbled on the floor, hardly room to walk in here, shoeboxes stacked to the ceiling. By the time I was dressed, I was exhausted. And there was still housework. More decisions. Dishes? Laundry? Gardening? So many tools and supplies to clean, sweep, dust, polish, repair, wax, scrub, mop. So many things that needed something done to them. Couches. Dressers and tables. Porcelain figures and wooden fruit. Hundreds of books. Fireplace tools, baskets, brass. Chandeliers. So many things. None of which I had chosen.

One day…the last decision I ever made…I called the Salvation Army. Had it all taken away. Kept a bowl, a spoon, and a cup. And what you see here. Now I'm really free. Free from decisions.

This rope? Here on the door handle? Remember the TV show about the pioneer family? They lived on the prairie. Remember in the winter they tied a rope between their cabin and the barn? That way…when there was a blizzard…they could feed their livestock without getting lost. When I have to leave my closet, my rope guides me to the bathroom and the kitchen—even with my eyes closed. That way I'm never lost. Lost in freedom.

I only leave when I have to, though. I'm never happier than here. My back to the wall. Door safely shut against your world and its bewildering choices. That bare bulb hanging there my sun and moon, the ceiling my sky. For windows, my imagination. I need nothing else. I'm afraid it's time for you to go now. Your visits exhaust me. Thank you for coming. See you next year.

SuzAnne C. Cole

Directions

something
is humping
its mother
in the woods

her only seeds
are stones
released
in a black lava

listen

to where
we are going:

a geology
of dark birth

Anne Coray

Sellout

when you sell your world
to the twinge of office time-warp,
then you know the reason clouds
disperse into the gloom of maelstrom;
you can walk through the thorns born
of the lesson, lie down in the gray and bitter
matter of its making and let the buzzards
pick your brain grayer than the gray it posted
on the thin furtive layer of success;

your own heartsong is the first thing they
ravish; your soul, the last.
soon you are the ghost you never thought
you'd cherish, staggering sideways
between the undercurrent of your hungry kids
vs. the arresting vacuum of your pulsing job;
and before you give in either way, the
hip-hop buzz you choose will be your life…

S. Soil

Career Guy Poem

Is the gesture of giving praise
to each new day sun diminished
by its routine by its lack
of originality

after a thousand times
it might have become mechanical
shortly after Cain's rock
"under light bulb luminescence"

became the answer to fire's
disobedient tongue
that howls against chain gang horizon
powerline rail tie

powerline rail tie
towers steeples rooftops
the air snagged in antennae
trapped in elevator hands

and elevator manicures
razor legs and razor jaws whispering
"fiduciary wings" and "fiduciary wax"
could I praise anything
in earnest besides the traffic helicopters
like dragonflies circling
the bridges and nearly kissing
the towerglass come five

Max Roland Ekstrom

Twilight Sleep

Twilight zone drugs down the hatch blow-up witch you are
a metaphor for wind in leaves of hope you will wear a straw hat
and drink stem cell glassed wine on icy melt-down scenarios…
We shall be dining in the OUTBACK with marsupial mountains;
keeping things warm in oven of appearances the powerful ruling
class covets will not stop at murder she said ok you can walk all
over like a doormat going to jail will not happen to big shots
ladling out spinach and pork shish kabobs in sauce in the city.
Down at harbor too many swans for lack of space developers
have developed the world wide planet middle east disaster ring
the dinner bell barbecuing chicken and frozen far away menus
reading Mexico, Chinese, international array in freezer they tell you
to stick in peppers for twenty minutes will soon be bed time
with the scent of cooking through a window you are ready for it
to be back on a radio because TV is so bad to tell the truth.
BS on main stream gibberish it is time to read again…oh please
let's not do Marilyn Monroe again….and endless reruns of real
war and lies let us hide in gossip columns before the local nuclear
plant blows us over the rainbow we know there is no escape route
city to the west ocean to the east you can only hunker down with
atoms. We live in a century of veiled threats and averted eyes in flags.
Humanity is slowly sinking into quicksands of complacency outside
of this aluminum sided 1911 house they are boxed dinners awaiting
butchering while the poor starve and the elderly and children shrink
where experts converge to measure such things.

Joan Payne Kincaid

Surreal Estate

The idea was the brainchild of a creative real estate agent who lost her job when a projected sales boom fizzled. Because people balked at paying such exorbitant prices for land and because she never balked at believing in herself, she decided to sell small tracts of her body. Using an ironing board as a desk and a public telephone within ringing distance from her open window, she launched a successful cottage industry without even owning a cottage.

In the first month she sold a section north of her kidney to a client with kidney problems. He hoped someday to buy up the kidney itself. To a man with an ulcer she sold a winding tract along her intestines and got a good price because a major artery flowed nearby. An alcoholic wanted to purchase her entire liver but concerns over toxic levels from her sorority days caused him to reconsider the offer before the deal could be closed.

Still, the concept caught on and in six short months she sold nearly all the space surrounding her internal organs, not to mention her right breast which a Freudian psychiatrist in New York leased with an option to buy simply because he liked the looks of it.

She was a businesswoman with astute market sense, and she was a meadow filled with wildflowers. She was an entrepreneur and role model for independent women everywhere, and she was the earth itself. She was an investment, a view, a desire only a few men could walk away from.

David Feela

Feng Shui

just because
we spent

every quarter
we had

sold our double
bed and

kitchen table
with chairs

watched as the gold Oldsmobile
was repossessed

leaving us stranded in
the desert west of Las Cruces

in a trailer
with no electricity

rent unpaid and
a landlord who threatened

to shoot us
tonight

don't even think I
have given
up

my peacock feather
is in the right

sector

and the lid
is down

Sheryl L. Nelms

Watching the TV Version of the Holocaust

Just when the mother was being shoved
with the rest toward the cattle car
bound for Auschwitz, and her daughter,
in the midst of the chaos and panic,
grabbed for the sleeve of her coat,
a young, smoothfaced woman with
the eyeshadow appeared and showed
how effective a little makeup could be.

Just as the son who had joined
the Czech partisans was about to kill a person
for the first time—another young boy
in a Nazi uniform, shoot him in the face
with a submachine gun—
the family in their large, brightly
lit bathroom got to quarreling about
toothpastes, but a new perfect toothpaste
resolved the issue.

The mother and father knew they would soon
be smoke and cinders emerging from that
distant chimney. The artist son was tortured,
and his wife had to fuck the prison guard
in order to get messages to her husband.
And just then the housewife told us
we could get rid of stains and odors
and make sure nothing stuck to the inside of the dryer.

Lou Lipsitz

The Silver Lining

While they lie, most of them, still, under the rubble,
Waiting, waiting for the eternal to come out in them,
The dead consider the news:

The insurance industry will, of course, absorb enormous losses, at first.
(An appeal for some sort of government bail-out is being considered.)
In the long run, however, the Twin Towers Tragedy might prove a
       tremendous boost to the engine of insurance:

The cost, (financial), we are told, may be added to the base-figure
       of the premium,
Thereby, in the long-long run, perhaps eternally,
Ensuring greater profits, praise Allah, praise Mammon.

David E. Williams

The History of the Twenty-First Century

We awoke, each day, accelerated. America was spent
with mornings still brilliant, but too small.
Television was what held the country together—
each of us the star of our own series.
We woke up and found our problem was that we always
lived in one world, but imagined another.
The most real things about us were our toys.
While we were trying to be Europe,
Europe was working to be us. We awoke
and saw we could never discover
Paris in Paris, could never
be Americans in America.
Forced to redefine the personal threshold, we took
the architecture of the past, disassembled
the built frontier to create a new one.
It isn't that we were escaping.
We were just leveling time,
seeing our faces fresh in the unfamiliar.
A nation that believes its own mythology
is doomed, so we became
historians of zero,
the pure flatness of that.
We went back to the nature of origin—*ours*,
and borders that, for once, set on expanse again.
A nation of escapees, we fled the idea of nationality.
The only frontier remaining rested on our chests.
What unified us was a final longing
for what we couldn't achieve.
When we saw our accomplishments over, what was left
was to repeat ourselves—so we embraced
the beauty of self-anarchy, its wiped colour.
We sculpted deserts out of cities.
We wanted a land of exactly noon, a place
of least shadow.
We heated everything
down to nova
and turned off the generators.
Heady with exile, we left
the doors open,
the wind drifting and touching
nothing.
We went for whiteness.

Nicholas Samaras

Career

Another night enclosed in concrete.
Do waves lap a rowboat tied to a dock
and a German shepherd sit on guard, eager
as the moon-engraved lake for my return?

An electronic box on my desk signals
the year nears zero. Weary from work
I watch wild geese silhouetted against
a full moon: framed, hanging on the wall.

Edward Beatty

Factory Ecstasy

Against a factory skyline
her arms Minoan snake sway.
Soft dance, dream heavy
smoke leaves earth. Sun-drunk
moon-round, names of lovers
swirl around her, patchouli
aromatic arms, palms open
pleasure. Freedom
and seduction under
her tongue.
Hiss
of second shift whistle
trespass thirty minutes of ecstasy.
Hiding her arms in her uniform
she pauses to bite
the last apple peel of sky
before a conveyer belt casts passion
into pipes and plastic.

Karen Howland

Call to Communion

My Father's house has many workstations,
prospects aplenty, countless customers
ready to buy;
and yea though ye die
ye shall achieve something
that sounds sort of like eternal life
through faithful execution
of a rock-solid business perpetuation plan.
(At least this life may *seem* an eternity.)
So come,
eat of the bread of sales,
drink of the wine of profits.

Daniel Hunter

From the Museum of Natural History

We're not chameleons, that's for sure;
we don't adapt—how ridiculous, absurd.
Our surroundings must fit us;
We live in the comfort zone:
our cars, a breath of cool air;
our bilevels, warm as toasterovens.
We need our bigmacs
      reddye #2
      colored charmin
      barbiedolls
      colortv
      trashmashers
      disposals
      blowdriers
      crockpots

paper products, more varied than trees,
tinfoil, more shining than mountains.
Until one day
on a sixlane
limited access
straightaway,
we all run out
of gas,
of time.
The planet cools down,
and we've sucked our last
sweet drop of crude.
We don't hear the long, slow
singing of our blood,
but stare, bewildered
at the neonless night:
the stars and their awful glare,
the air, thin and cruel
on our furless skin,
the moon, obscenely white
and unreachable.

We wander,
until we lose all ways,
sink into the tar,
and dream the last dream.

Until our relics
are unearthed
and repostured
beside a winnebago
(reconstructed)
in a diorama
on seventy-ninth street.

Barbara Crooker

Our Conscience

Of course we fear that aliens from space
will invade Earth and take over our world.
Their skin will be a different color,
they will use weapons that are more advanced
than anything we have, and we will be powerless
to stop their assaults on our cities.

Our conscience hasn't forgotten how we
stole this country from Native Americans,
marched them at gunpoint to reservations,
slaughtered their buffalo,
built dams that killed salmon,
spread smallpox and measles.

Our conscience remembers how we
bound Africans in chains,
shipped them across the ocean like animals,
whipped them to do our work,
sold their children at auctions,
cut off their limbs if they tried to escape.

No wonder we're paranoid that alien beings
would force us to assimilate,
to change the way we dress and how we talk.
They'd outlaw our customs, reduce our culture
to an exhibit in their history museum,
down the hallway across from the restrooms.

Mary Laufer

On the Planet Logo

You stitch together footgear
While sealed in all day
In a sweat box
Behind padlocked doors,
From childhood
To old arthritic age.

When your eyes no longer see
And your fingers can no longer stitch,
You go out the back door
With the discards
To die.

Your life's work is shipped off-world
And sold, for what would be to you
A fortune, freedom, and
The children of other worlds
Kill each other
Just to possess their intoxicating power,

Which allows them to believe, for a time,
That they will not end with the discards,
Nor live their lives in a box
Of certain dimensions.

David E. Williams

Collections of Nearly Unlovable Spaces

In this Arboretum I've got Bare Ground Sickness, understory
        withdrawal.
The thing that writes itself here could be fire, burning the
        pattern of a catamount print.

No interpretive signage says: "Chinese Railroad Worker was
        hung from this Live Oak."
Places and pasts are simultaneous places and times in the open
        mind.

A cluster of us won't leave the hills, fog, bored mule deer and
        pre-fab homes.
I blame the addictive water we drank as kids, laced with traces
        of quicksilver.

Phases of the madrone tilting into cold nights. Hard green
        berries begin to blush.
String them up from Memory's throat, her breath a vanilla
        drench of evening blossoms.

What we are (a boy) practicing (was hanged) is suffering
        (here),
which everybody practices, but strangely few grow graceful in.

Kids throwing rocks at ducklings. Kids pitching stones
        between ducks.
White shank of egret neck against green water.

Wells, pipes, wires get "shrubbed up"—architect's slang for
        hidden.
Codes for not resisting red penstemon blooms got shrubbed up
        in the hands of my son.

Tule fog, no guarantees on middle distance; animals bounce
        echoes off each other's hides.
Over there, the well-motor grinding, or scrub jays shrieking like
        acorn-mad preachers.

Sinking fog, please spread the Gap(s) of Putahtoi.* A mall is
        the new river fork.
(Even in Putahtoi,
        tule fog damp in my hair,
                I long for Putahtoi.)

María Meléndez

*Source: Tony Hoagland. "Putahtoi" is Patwin for "Home at Putah Creek."

RiteAid

The brick is hurled through the window.
With the force delivered by a 95-pound boy
His arm pulled back over his head, into the RiteAid,
The brick lands 36 feet from me in glass shards.
A boom that punctures; the window gives way
Vomits on merchandise; the cashier screams
Her head is too close to where it entered. I'm in front
Of her; right side of my head glitters from broken glass
The retreating sun peers in, sees customers running
Down the aisles. I hunch in front of nail clippers and
            Twizzlers.
The boy is gone, hurled the brick with his 95-pound body,
Through a window, and he's practicing what he knows
Of openings created by things hurled by heavy bodies;
He's familiar with the sound that follows; he knows
About how things collapse beneath the force of an object
Thrown against another object that is once whole and he
Knows that when something receives a blow it tries
With all its might to hold together. But when a brick,
A fist, a shoe, a belt, a serrated insult, anything solid
And accessible, light enough to lift and hard enough to hurt
Is thrown at something weaker, it breaks open and stays
            exposed
Until someone pays attention. And he knows that some
Wounds are too big to heal on their own, it needs
Assistance to repair itself, otherwise left unattended it will
Fester, ferment, spread until toxins tunnel through his
Veins; he knows that wounds become black holes hidden
On his black skin, and so he stands in front of RiteAid,
Making the only thing he knows how: a hole.

Arisa White

62

Valiant Soldiers
(perennials)*

*Please follow planting instructions for your combat zone.

This strain matures at an early 13 years.
Each Valiant Soldier produces guaranteed offshoots
and year after year of hardy kill-resistant stock.

For a good yield work the soil well,
infiltrating it liberally with bone meal and desiccated blood.
Stake supports of barbed wire, digging shallow trenches
                                                        along the rows.
Plant the shells at equal intervals with the Soldiers
so they will come up in uniform drills.
Cover the soil and wait for the reign of terror.
Remove and promptly exterminate slugs.
Your crop should advance at the first sign of provocation.

Valiant Soldiers especially thrive on heat,
but will adapt readily to every clime and terrain.
Cut them down to the quick for a continuous supply.

Pests and Diseases:

The bullet fly. The mourning dove. The yellow fungus.
For control of native weed population, spray between drills.
Your grandfather loved Valiant Soldiers so much
he took them out West! Now, decades later, you
can enjoy the same homegrown riots of khaki.
A continual Presidential choice for monumental
plantings in historic Soldier's Field.
Whether for swamp beds or 6-foot borders
Valiant Soldiers have long been a favorite the world over.

Each shipment government inspected and approved.

Julia Older

The Eagle

In the chill orange light
of the suggestion of fires
our leaders are convening.
They are meeting
like a field in a wind,
and hush, or stir, or part
with the ache of great reluctance.
Listen to the cry.
One of the leaders is remembering.
He remembers America.
He remembers himself.
He was as fine
and as polished as a Chrysler.
He insists. He demands.
He says
"We didn't say shit."
And who is to say.

Across everything there is silence.
Nothing done, nothing said.
Who wants anyone to die.
Who wants anyone killed.
Only a child—and so young,
he won't say it.
He is dying.
All he thinks of is living.
Sometimes he can only perspire.
The country is swelling in him.
He is ready to fall open.
He is ready for the one cold night
his breath escapes him
and trembles in the air,
and is an eagle,
and is what is being done to him,
and is what killed him.

Dennis Saleh

Valentine in Red, Black and Blue

February 14, 2002 George Bush declares war against the planet,
unleashing his energy plan.

The stripes have turned to black and blood,
drip lines on a ripping standard,
lines like blind alleys,
etched by the magnet of ego,
straight lines determined long ago,
unwritten lines between those penned,
"destroy and overcome, even the earth."

Blue gangrene creeps up the corpse
of the planet that could have been.
Each star bursting in air
gives proof of our allegiance
to destruction,
ego fortified by greed,
ego encouraged by compulsion,
ego unhampered by reflection.

But there in the abyss of the explosion
lies the path to wholeness, holiness.
That dark hollow hides white truth.

Take the turn into the unknown,
curving, dark, mysterious.
Take it.

Rema Boscov

Government at Work

Buried in the estate tax section of the big tax-cut bill the House of Representatives plans to approve is an obscure provision that would cost the Government $9 million a year in lost revenue and give a bonanza worth thousands of dollars to about 1000 wealthy taxpayers.

The officials say it's a mystery
how the windfall provision got into the bill.
They were not approached
by constituents, contributors, or lobbyists.
No one claims authorship.

Did the windfall provision get in by mistake?
Implausible, say the officials.
The Treasury is familiar with the windfall issue.
It's been circling for years, so lucrative
to so few (but who the few are, no one knows).

And what is the windfall issue?
Something to do with trust throwback rules
in the tax code, actually, tax shelters
(now we understand) called
multiple trusts, no longer legal.

The officials agree the rules are arcane,
raise little revenue and should be repealed.
But if they are scrapped indiscriminately
(as the House Bill would do)
then there is the side effect of the windfall.

Side effects are not something one thinks
of as having to be arranged,
at least, not medicinally speaking.
The officials agree the side effect had to be
specifically written into the bill.

Everyone agrees that somewhere somebody
got to someone and nobody is telling who they are.

Helen Tzagoloff

Found in Dave's Things

Dear Bank of America
I must admit first of all
that I am very pleased
with your service. It is
an entirely pain free ad-
mission and one I take
great joy in making. I do
realize that this could be
construed as just a letter
from a lonely customer
with nothing better to do
than spend his free
time writing to banks
and while that is not
entirely untrue let me
also say that I do appreciate
the courteous helpful treatment
I have received from
each branch.

Rick Smith

Incantation

I am in prayer! I tell myself tonight,
my body returning me from my fall
through windows in myself I never saw
a way out of until this minute.
And now I'm back and still alive.
I wish I could tell you the Christmas music
carried me on wings a few seconds back
looping through DayGlo wreaths and Santa Claus
who appeared every few feet above the door of each shop,
a tiny god the shoppers looked up to as they passed.
I wish I could tell you I was only trembling
because it was Christmas Eve, when I would be received
by my wife and children in an hour, protected,
and be at home in myself with them
whose warming breath would take me in.
This would, yes, come to pass, but for the moment
which is this poem I am only grateful
the star had come and stood, cocked above my head
and passed me over: a salesclerk with a .38
had opened fire on children queuing up
to whisper last minute wishes in St. Nick's ear.
They are all dead; their little bodies like game birds
all six spread out, then carted off by three janitors
now scrubbing down the blood-streaked floor.
Who am I praying for, the dead or me or passersby
who have no reason to be among the living
any more than you, reader, or the man, handcuffed, gagged
who may be loose within a year to surprise one of us
but not me, we think, mumbling the old words
as I did, beginning this, words catching on my tongue
and if we're lucky, invoking someone.

Peter Cooley

Hearing the Echo

Spend a rainforest on a hamburger.
Spend an ozonelayer on a refrigerator.
Spend a mountainrange to buy an electric range.
Spend a thousand-year-old tree on disposable
         chopsticks.
Spend a generation of young men in World War I
         so World War II won't happen.
Buy a tuna sandwich with a slaughtered dolphin.
Buy an airconditioner with a runaway Greenhouse Effect.
Spend the Great Lakes to possess a Jacuzzi.
Spend the best years of a humanbeing's life in a factory
         as a factoryworker praising your job
                  while your great-great grandfather's
         boyorgasmcries wait for you
                  to hear the echo of their echo.
Purchase furcoats with deathcries
         of endangered species.
Spend the suspended sentences of execution
         to deathrow inmates
                  on exciting new advertising
         for skyrocketing cigarette sales
                  in Third World countries.
Spend the astonished look of delight in a baby's eyes
         on car-bombs that disfigure
                  the unsuspecting victim.
Spend the vows of lifelong love
         made by a boy and girl
                  on new improved body bags
         for our dead soldiers
                  that are guaranteed
         not to leak or burst.

Antler

Seeds

You were the grubby kid next door
who became a criminal.

And yet when you were seven I discovered
your hidden garden near the brook out back.
Screened by brambles, frail Shirley poppies
fluttered pale chiffons by leathery marigolds.
I knew that you had stolen the seeds.

You knelt beside a knife-straight row,
drizzling water with a rusty lid.
When you saw me, your face turned fierce.
"Don't tell my dad!" you snarled. "Get outa here!"

Next day I brought a potted mum and a picture.
"It will look like this." Mutinous, you glared.
Then you gazed at the plant and I saw heart-hunger.

In February I showed you a seed catalog.
"Pick twelve kinds you want. I'll order them."
That spring I worried. You swaggered with our
town's young bullies. Yet the flowers nurtured you.
I dared to hope that somehow you would bloom.

One summer evening I heard screams.
Running to the plot, I saw your father
stomp larkspur flat, rip out fringed pinks.

Later, face down in churned-up soil,
you sobbed into tatters of ruined blossoms.
I rubbed your bony back. "Don't give up!
You have a gift. You'll find a way."

In time, weeds overtook the patch. Your family
moved away. Before long I saw your name
in the court news. Heartsick, I recalled
how small fingers had nursed frail seedlings.

Last I heard, you were in prison. For years,
no word. Then, tonight on TV, the miracle.
Clear-eyed, standing tall, you lead reporters

through the home you run for delinquent teens.
Outside, your arm sweeps over grounds
gorgeous with flowers. "Garden therapy works
wonders," you say. "The kids did all of this."

Tears come as I remember rose silk poppies
beside a sheltered stream.

Dalene Stull

Real Abundance

Henry comes by in an orange vest, takes away the milk cartons after I've milked them, takes away the **Pepperidge Farm** box and double wrapping, bloody pork roast **Styrofoam** and soak pad and plastic, **Betty Crocker** au gratin potato package, and he takes the pre-peeled mini-carrots bag. (I wonder about the carrot-material that process peels away. I hope the grindings are bought for carrot cake mixes.)

Henry drives 20 miles from his home in a pickup truck he fills with gas, assures the oil's changed, stops by **Speedway** for coffee he doesn't brew himself and drinks from a toss-away cup. He gets to Newark where he clocks in at **Waste Management**. He makes good on the promise to be at our house 17 miles away by 5 o'clock every Wednesday morning to take it all away. Take what? This stuff our stuff comes in, this stuff that causes displeasure with its appearance, its smell, its lack of usefulness any longer. Henry works to make me comfortable, to get a dumpster's-worth a week out of my life, things I find no further use for: **Duncan Hines** boxes (mother made cakes from scratch); rubberbands off newspapers, newspapers, seven 2-liter softdrink bottles I refuse to cut in two to start tomato seeds in because they are unsightly. Henry (you know Henrys too) leaps on and off his street-wise grinding behemoth and marathons 50 blocks a day our mass destruction of resources, tosses the equivalent of 200 elephants with his bare hands into his movable tent, dumps years of **Xeroxing** I don't need after all, manila folders inside hanging files, pens that hold so little ink I've used some only twice. Their casings accompany **Tropicana** cartons to the trash because I don't squeeze oranges or lemons nor find uses for their rinds like they do on the **Food Network**.

When I was a child I was dreamy-eyed and insightful, could see the whole world turn turn turn earth without blue tubs for paper and red for metal at curbside. Milk came in glass never discarded. We put out empties that **Borden Milk Company** scalded to refill, left again on our steps the following Tuesday out of the sun in a dark cool box. Two cents for every **Coke** bottle return bought me a pair of mittens and nothing additional in the trash. Soft drinks, milk, diapers, and dusting never involved throwing anything away.

My neighbor fills the dump **Swiffer** than she did last year—
excited about a new disposable mop. She has one baby in **Pampers**
and one in the new disposable training pants. **Bounty** soaks the spills.
Who has time to remove buttons and zippers from old shirts to use as
rags, wash out, and use again? I do but I choose not to with the excuse
that I work 20 hours a day already. Commercials fool us into thinking
we have less time nowadays but we all have 24 hours and make our
choices.

I open an antique sideboard, finger Irish linens unused in 30
years. Guest towels are "linen quality" paper now. **Hallmark** paper
plates tower on the counter then into **Glad Bags** leaf-mound high
because of a few sandwich crumbs or a piece of cake.

In church we pray for abundance and when it comes we throw
it away, we pray for deliverance though we are our own transport, we
pray to be saved but don't learn how to save. Get it messy and take
it away—the sun comes up again. Fifty more crackers are double-
sealed for freshness though they're loaded with preservatives.
Everything is engineered for obsolescence: refrigerators, washing
machines, televisions, even our **Pepsi** has an expiration date now and
actually loses that fizz more quickly than it used to.

Today I baked a batch of chocolate chip cookies (that's 42) sent
half next door to people I don't know. They *will return the glass plate
on Saturday* they said as though struggling to speak a foreign language.
My note to them says *Thank you for that mass of tulips outside my
library window.* It's scratched in ink drawn from the **Scripto** bottle
into a fountain pen I refill. Tomorrow could I bring myself to act like
this again? And then another day, and another? *Don't make promises
you can't keep*, my wiser self whispers. *One day at a time* my
dedication seems more doable. Today there is no end to blessings.

Jennifer Bosveld

Souls Like Mockingbirds

The mockingbird on my block
is doing car alarms again.
He doesn't have much choice.
Unlike his country cousins,
his options for mockery are somewhat
limited—
sparrows, starlings, crows…
and car alarms.

I would love to say
that he reclaimed the
horrible human noise
insult to the air
invader of private spaces
and made it something of nature again,
strangely beautiful.

But actually it's still damn ugly
when he does it
nah-nee nah-nee nah-nee
whooop, whooop, whooop
enh, enh, enh
He passes it through like an
unchewed kernel of corn
telling about his world
letting no one forget what is going on
absorbing nothing
keeping his soul intact.

We do the same.
We talk back to the TVs and the billboards
because it's only the final word
that gets inscribed on our hearts.

We tell all the stories of pain and powerlessness
that we cannot leave on the doormat
when we come home
because if we speak their lessons full volume

they cannot whisper their hopelessness
in our ears.

The pressure of too much ignoring
forces the grit of what should not be
deep into our shoulder blades
turning them to brittle steel.

So we too
echo the car alarms,
around the dinner table
trying to remember
the order of the different
alarm sounds,
searching out a
rhythm in the
insistence to
drum with our
hands on our
thighs.

We have
souls like mockingbirds.
Loud.
Ever open.
And (almost) intact.

Miriam Axel-Lute

Devolution

I am ready to crawl
on my naked belly.
If psychoanalysis is where
the winds of evolution
have borne this seed,
then I'd rather
stroke my ignorance
down on the mudflats,
in and out of the water
with the newts, with the frogs,
communing with the buttercups
where they paint
the trees at dawn.
I am ready to lose
these legs,
grow flippers.
I am weary of walking up stairs
to cramped offices,
of explaining where I come from
when it's really all about
where we all come from.
Lovers, family...
give me instinct and the egg.
I want to buzz
under the lily pad,
suck the sacred milk
from nameless antecedents,
live and die
as if there's nothing inbetween.
It's the self,
I pay this blind gypsy to tell me.
Well the self,
if the winds are gentle
and the temperature just right,
can go lose its mind
and still be sane.

John Grey

What Has Been Lost

The ability to reenvision desire, puzzle of the self,
map to the territory of the unlived life.

Star-wishes, the courage to step on a crack.

How to speak with innocence,
sit at someone's feet, follow deer through underbrush,
how to apologize and mean it.

Baby teeth in the silk pouch,
the scientist who wrote his own obituary,
Father and his father, the delicate touch of a fingertip,
the diamond pin, the right breast.

Art of paddling whitewater or stanching blood.
How to guide a marionette, rub sticks for fire.
How to make one kiss matter.

The range of freedom. What the golden eagle might tell
about pursuit and betrayal.

The day foxes come from their dens
and salamanders from under their rocks.

Dream of rising from bed, flying along through night cirrus.

Songs flung to the air, greedy and heedless,
exhaling measures of love.

The fugitive meaning of tomorrow and next year.

The sexual jolt of the earthquake and its aftershocks.
How to decode other voices of the wild
whispering from marsh and river and sea.

All this relinquished, bargaining, bargaining,
bargaining for ease instead of edge,

tired of waiting for the ninth wave, for the chrysalis,
for the epiphany of an unexpected morning.

Susan Terris

II. Breaking the Spell

Discipline

after Wendell Berry

Wake up. Begin to see.
There is despair, yes. It stinks.
Do not move away from it as if
it were a dead and rotted thing
you can ignore. It reeks only of
ego and hubris—humankind
so arrogant to believe itself
indestructible, to believe
Earth an unlimited warehouse
instead of a home.
Take despair into your arms. Don't be afraid.
Hold it tight, admit it as part of you.
dance with it, and, as you dance,
it will grow less awful, lighter—
so light that you can finally release it
and begin to act.

Nita Penfold

Why Should I Care

Because, whatever else lies in us, we humans
have always known deeply to turn
our moist branching lungs as outside in, inside out offering
back to the grand silent exhalation of forests
that gives itself molecule by molecule
to the intricate treeing miles
of our billionfold bodies' red sap and flow.

Because we already honestly have been and are
the old-growth wisdom named *Symbiosis*:
a living with: the tacit grateful intelligence
that plays its geotime and milliseconds between
the give-and-take twined surfaces of our capillaries
and the gently dilating and closing stomata of leaves.

Because meanwhile, garishly, the one, the only, the
        out-of-joint ego,
is plundering its very last robbery and sequestering of our
        breath to curse
go on, get lost, it's just Greek to me
slashing and chopping itself as it does,
itself and all else human, all else tree, down and away as it does
into the impervious coffin of solely its own making.

Mary Krane Derr

Valentine, After September 11

Let the heart crack.
Let it form a hollow like a beggar's upraised bowl.
Let it be a cistern for sobs.

Let the heart embrace the grief
become a womb,
a sac to gestate heart-ears and heart-eyes
that hear and see the sobbing of all other hearts.

Let the tears become a lake,
a balm, a placid pool,
all of us on its shore
cupping both hands,
bending toward the water to drink.

Rema Boscov

Breaking the Spell

Weary of sadness and loss, in shock perhaps, isn't it easy to simply pretend that all is well? Billions of dollars are spent to shield us from the truth, to support the very structures that blind us to what is truly happening in America. Modern technological culture feeds on the memory loss of our origins, and it is not easy to fight our way back upstream. And what's more, our forgetting has been so purposeful and systematic that we forget that we have forgotten! Ironically, in our Age of Information we are missing the information most vitally important to us: how to dwell in community with each other and the natural world.

Studies within the burgeoning field of ecopsychology can help tremendously in identifying the impacts of our dysfunctional relationship with nature—a relationship that has been building to a crescendo since the Industrial Revolution.   The basic tenet of ecopsychology is that the vast majority of psychoses and neuroses afflicting the modern human are a reflection of our fragmented relationship with nature. The state of our environment continually mirrors itself in our interior lives, in ways that are difficult to recognize. We then perpetuate the crisis with self-destructive behavior, because we feel so terrible under the surface of our lives. Any "cure" to this vicious circle lies within our ability to break free by developing a more reciprocal relationship with the natural world. For this to happen, our definition of sanity must literally be redefined. This is the goal of ecopsychology.

"What we do to the Earth, we do to ourselves." These words attributed to northwest native elder Chief Seattle have always been a beacon of our recovery and can lead us away from the addictive compulsions of an unsustainable society.

As we try to patch together the shards of our distorted relationship with nature, "we often regress, slipping away from the world, hiding and peering from the very crack that initiates recovery," writes ecopsychologist Laura Sewell in *Sight and Sensibility: The Ecopsychology of Perception*. It hurts to awaken to the outrage and trauma of what is happening to Earth. It hurts to acknowledge our unwitting complicity in the undoing of Mother Gaia and the shame that comes with it. Our sensory systems are highly evolved and the pain of it all is extremely difficult to bear (one reason anti-depressants are so widely prescribed).   Through it all, it is important that we have compassion for ourselves and our need to protect our spirit from the terror of what is happening. Always, we must forgive ourselves and then, look a second time. We must look again and again and muster the courage to stop pretending, to face despair and resist the urge to give in sleepily to the seductions and superficial comforts of modern society.

"Fear of despair," writes deep ecologist Joanna Macy in *World As Lover, World As Self*, "can erect an invisible screen selectively filtering out anxiety-provoking data. In a world where organisms require feedback in order to adapt and survive, this is suicidal." The pain we carry for our imperiled world is only dysfunctional when we refuse to own it. In the not-so-very-long run, it is our wakefulness, our facing of what haunts us, that contains our brightest chance as a species.

In the midst of these apocalyptic times, we must learn to dwell with an open heart—with eyes and ears and spirits wide open. To stay present amid ecological ruin and numbing propaganda is a spiritual discipline. Hope for ourselves and the world resides in this practice. Any chance of influencing the human outcome rises first from accepting the truth. When we honor our grief for the world, we approach the wisdom and joyful fit that is our birthright—a deep and soulful recognition of our oneness with Earth. Is this the intent behind the old Irish prayer to be alive at the end of history? May you be alive when the spell is broken, at the beginning of *our* story—a time when humanity has rediscovered how to live in balance with Earth and each other. And most importantly, the prayer seems to say, "*Realize the special gift that you have to offer the world and learn to wield it.*"

How can we unearth the unique gifts that we each have to offer the world at this critical time? How do we maintain our courage? How do we balance the joy and rage inherent in the awareness of being "alive at the end of history"? We each must find a way, or risk slipping back into the allure of the pretending spell. In her lectures and workshops, spiritual ecologist Sister Miriam MacGillis offers a profound solution. "What can help us," she says, "is that instead of asking what we can do to change the world, we must ask as well, *what can we do to bless it.*" Here, I believe, lies the secret of real change: grounding our actions with direct and personal displays of our devotion to Earth.

Daniel Dancer

Shelling Peas

"That's one of those traditional things Torie and Peggy do while they are enjoying their break from housekeeping."
—Martha Stewart

When there is nothing left to do,
squirrels race around trees. Bet
on the winter. Revise ideas about
birds and water after watching
a hundred wrens chabbling in baths
one scorching afternoon.
Keep the feeders stocked with seed
by day and meat for the night eaters.
Dead-head the marigolds for more
marigolds. Pinch back the basil.
Train the morning glorys to follow,
not just climb, the lattice of wire
webbing the antenna. Do not
leave anything to chance. Do
not go in the house. Salvage
the volunteers: tomato tragically
next to rue. Even the paving stones
upended by spruce roots. Blow
into the poppy's center. Sweep
the patio. Snap off dry raspberry
canes. Bend new growth arching
toward the bee balm. Wick moisture
from the crane pitcher with
rolled up paper towel. Crumble
sage in your smelly running shoe.
Learn the bird songs. Sing them
accompanied early in the morning
but avoid entering the house where
things are waiting for you to do.

Elizabeth Kerlikowske

Acedia

Twelve years old, my boyfriend's son can't find
    anything to do. Keeps staring at the empty page
of his Sunday as if by returning enough times to
    the kitchen where I sit writing he'll say *yes!* discover
it filled. Inside you, I want to tell him, a shaman
    sings fiercely over twigs—out of Nothing, golden
fire—and this flame curling upward in your chest,
    self-created, is named pleasure; look, I almost say,
on black-star afternoons when the world collapses
    to the size of your head, when your baseball, PS2
and skateboard have lost all power to please you,
    blow hard into the Void. Michael, breathe life in.

Ellen Wehle

Star-Struck Utopias of the 21st Century

What if Society became so obsessed with the stars
          as a result of Emerson's epiphany
"If the stars came out only one night in a thousand years
          how people would believe and adore
                    and preserve from generation to generation
          remembrance of the miracle they'd been shown"
That everyone started sleeping during the day
          so they could stay up all night
                    star-gazing, star-thinking, star-dreaming.
Being in the Milky Way so they could have
          maximum exposure to the Universe
                    beyond Earth and our own Star.
Rather than being consumed by human history,
          art, literature, music, religion, politics, business,
                    consumed by the stars,
          hunger to be with them and
                    star-roving Milky Waydom,
So much so that people spent more time
          looking at the Milky Way than at each other,
                    more time looking up
          than straight ahead or down.
Total blackout in all cities—no streetlights, stoplights, carlights
          driving at night illegal,
                    no lights in buildings but candles,
Whole populations thronging to darkened
          stadiums and skyscrapertops
                    to sit holding hands en masse
          and look up at the billion-year spree
                    of the realm of the nebulae!

Antler

Absence of Benign Deprivation

What you kids need is a good depression, my mother said,
undone by the abundance her grace of simple living
seemed powerless to overcome. Her words intrigued us
even as we held them up to ridicule.
What if that mysterious "good" in the Great Depression
were something we might have to do without?

Now to our own children we say inexplicable things.
And we can give them everything but what they truly need—
the shaping form of need itself,
the expectant concave gesture of emptiness,
the thing they long for as I craved peaches when pregnant.
While we fill their walls with art, their hours with lessons,
their rooms with toys, their heads with wisdom,
their ears with quality music (in Dolby surround-sound),
their fantasies have them orphaned, begging in the streets.

Take our daughter, loved and lavished
by two parents and a house full of brothers.
She's quick to pretend herself a lonely waif, building
a cottage of cardboard or forming shelter among the trees,
adorning barren surroundings with found objects,
surviving on forest berries or singing for sustenance.
Fairy tales of street children spark her imagination
like no princess stories.
The Little Match Girl feeds her hunger to be hungry.
Her mind is most active in conjuring lack,
putting up a tent village on the verdant, tree-lined streets of
her neighborhood, peopling it with cripples and beggars and
gaunt, mythic mothers with many babies nursing them thin.
In her "pretends" she finally bands with capable, independent
children like herself who can build amid the ruins.
They begin to form a heart's home
out of dreams and nothingness.

Maureen Tolman Flannery

if it ain't been in a pawn shop

if it ain't been in a pawn shop
if goodwill didn't tag it
if it wasn't dickered down
for pocket change at a yard sale

if it hasn't been loaded
and unloaded
from some stranger's
rusted out '72 ford pickup
parked at a flea market

if it's shrinkwrapped
in virgin plastic
and smells of formaldehyde
insecticide
fungicide
or windex with ammonia-d

if the upc code is scanned
by an expensive laser
which belongs to a computer
which belongs to a
corporate billion dollar logo
printed on t-shirts
made in haiti
and worn by
urine-tested
god-fearing
flag-waving
fingerprinted
fifteen cents above minimum wage
slavebots

i'd rather avoid it
i'd rather not trust it
i'd rather wash the stains off
my thrift shop bargain
thankyou

and live with the blemishes
made accidentally
by other humans
unknown to me

i need a ragtag
recycled
secondhand
reincarnated
connection to my stuff
it's gotta have some
soul to it
it's gotta have a story
even if it's a secret
even if no one remembers
even if no one cares

i wanna look at my things
and know that
i can't pretend that
there is anything
new
in this world

Debra McCorkle Wells

Ways to World Peace

Have a garden
share its corners
with the wild rabbits

Thank the crow
for eating roadkill

Share a peace pipe
even if you fear
the germs left
in speckles of spit

Venerate teachers
who know they do
not know everything
suspect the teacher
who knows all

Beware the leader
who counts subjects
like a money lender
counts coins

Befriend your nightmares
they are your teachers

"Let honesty be
your divine power
and the absence of self
your sword"*

Honor the snake
the giver of the apple
it transmutes poison
to medicine, superstition
to wisdom, then
swallows its tail

Miriam Ben-Yaacov

from "Warrior's Creed" by Anonymous Samurai, 14th century

Their Gathering

For Darren Matthew and Brian David

My boys harvest from a mountain streamside
the remembering bones of this hour
green and wet, off by ourselves,
splashing and laughing: last season's
darkening acorns, twiggy sticks and straws of grass
washed down in spring flood, a small rock shaped,
they testify, like a Lego lost long ago;
they consider too a green-sided tree frog
only as big as a thumbnail
hopping from slick bank to tumbling water
with clear amphibian resolve,
then let it flee into its rippling peace.
At home, I know, they will set their treasures
in the place of treasures, alongside the older others,
and move, as boys do, ahead of memory
toward the next new light. Still
I pray they will recall, grown years from now,
this moment of endless gathering,
their surrender to water and earth
and a small frog's power,
even as their bodies race into manhood,
even as the world of zeroes orders them
to turn their backs on it all.

Robert Aquinas McNally

The Suggestion of Slivers

In this land of pampered abundance
bushes take their turns blossoming politely
shop windows shine
all colors stay vivid
What mistakes we make we can mop up
without muddying our hands
There are cushions for any awkward positions
should we find ourselves in them
on this Easy Street

Off-the-cuff actions garner no regrets
and our penchant for quenching
whatever might need it
is limited only
by imagination
Plump with possibility our hopes float
pleasantly scented
seamlessly presented

which is why weekly
I let the Frigidaire empty
and watch my children forage
through the remains:
brown rice leftovers
berries bruised in storage
the heels of bread
I want them to know barrels do have bottoms
and this is how they taste

Shoshauna Shy

Melting Into the World

for Matt Fox

Standing in line at Staples,
in front of me a mother
buying school supplies.
She has a stack of 3-hole loose-leaf,
some plastic binders, the requisite
pens, pencils, and erasers. Her face
is tense and tired and it all costs too
much for what she has to spend
this week, and for weeks to come.
I am fearful the loose-leaf will be
inscribed by her child's hand
with wrong answers, or right ones.
I know that somehow that sheet
after sheet after uniform sheet, with
all the blue lines so neatly spaced,
were trees once, and that's where
I'd like her and her kids to head,
to the living trees, to get the hell
out of this diminishment, to notice
when the bugs finally stop biting!
To live an autumn storm and if you
wanted to put something down
about the first frost, you could
do that, tracing with your little finger
on the window, writing with your
body's warmth,
melting into the world,
it into you. The story of now,
and none other.

Roger Davies

Making Play

Bambino,
little bear cub,
Your mother tells me
you are riding mops & brooms
& you have taken over
her container
of brightly colored clothespins.
You make music with pots & pans
and nesting toys out of measuring cups.
Let no one get you storebought toys.
May you go on, lifelong,
making play out of
what other people work at.

Karen Ethelsdattar

The Tempest

to my daughter Miranda

If you name your daughter *vision*,
or *wondrous to behold*, you should not be surprised
if she comes to you in anger or in shame,
wishing to be known as *Mary* or *Ann*.
That will be the moment to carry her out
to the things of the world she is not,
speaking other sounds that were almost hers:
aspen, lily-white, cumulo-nimbus glow.

Soon enough she'll realize the world,
too often, gets named in hope of profit,
or deceit, or the scientist's exactitude.
But on the greening island of the family
testing its voice in the months of waiting,
the sought-after words are music and the past:
Grandparent. Aunt. Child deceased.

Spirits of fashion and monsters of commerce
lurk, bedfellows eager to keep us
from our own best inventions and songs.
Some days it seems we grow from wailing silence
into speech, only that we might curse
the coming return to silence.
But if you've named your daughter *wondrous to behold*,
she'll someday learn she heard those words
before all others, and then again, and again.
When you are gone beyond all roaring
she'll know, should you ever brave return,
which words are the first you'll speak.

Stephen Corey

Speaking With Magpies

Out here I can say anything
        among the frozen apples
        and bird-pitted pears.

There is no one to hear me,
        yet if I tell a lie,
        the trees will crowd in
        to rub their barks against my tongue.

I watch the windmill in the field
        roll in its circling about the earth
        pulling up the waters
        for magpies and me.

We speak,
        the magpies and me.

We speak of what is important:
        black and white feathers
        orange eyes
        night
        twigs for nests.

We continue to speak:
        leaf mulch
        open gates
        dried grasses
        shadows of clouds.

We shall go to the mall,
        the magpies and me,
        we will speak with radiated tomatoes
        and beef marrow bones.

James McGrath

Desire

It takes time to listen to spring
walk among the trillium, lamb's tongue in the woods
large red tulips in the garden

to eat oatmeal for breakfast
drink brown rice tea, honeyed
amber-light of early sun.

Then the rain very heavy, a weight
of vernal equinox weeks past—
            what is not yet

though the hyacinth, violets,
cherry blossoms
swathe the air with moist scent

as longing sometimes does,
the desire to be unrestrained,
to show up, even dance

salsa or merengue
the fluidity of limbs, music
blood shimmering

as the petals of these enormous tulips
in the unexpected birth of light
death of shadow.

Gwen Morgan

Voyages

I.

Beneath a plastic defiance of gravity
In a jungle of coins and electric impulses
Through usury of city gutters
Passing around ghosts, tearing out hair
And the faces that cannot stop even
As summer slaves to death's wintry rage
In hawkish times when generations
Are still born to yank apart
And crack to forget
That one can actually live
Since speed is not all we are.

II.

There, in stillness, the timeless begins
Sacred, and, after many crossings, found:
Time for the birds of return,
Time for the revolution of wilderness,
Time for the wisdom of community,
Time for summers impassioned,
Time for breath richly-birthed.

It is time, it is time
To cultivate you and me
To farm the scale of vowels
Consonant with no-words
Whose thundering silence
Gallops up a newer mountain.

Richard Alan Bunch

Dreams Make Wishes In My Existence Of Thrift

Thrift: 1. healthy and vigorous growth
             2. careful management especially of money
             3. gainful occupation
             4. any of a genus (*Armeria*) of the plumbago family of
                    perennial evergreen acaulescent herbs

I am launching up,
stem-wise and vivid,
rooted in the lush soil of moments.
These acres of distinctions
living towards clarity,
breaking through the routine plasma,
and exposing me to new yearnings.
My existence of thrift
draws life from the veins of my stems
to fuel this journey;
these trials
of daring exploration
into the framework of soaring
heart and soul-stream translation.
Humbled, I am searching below
my limits to find
the birth of extraordinary normalcy.
I am delving into my experiences
to relive their spontaneous nature,
and to relieve my aching doubts,
by retracing the paths of my earthly practice,
the thruway of seams between
"body and soul."
My bones have grown new force to swell,
and finally give my faith a face.

Janna Willoughby

Poetry Mind

Poetry keeps my mind from being
standardized. Poetry mind not
standardized mind Poetry and mind
will not be standardized
Poetry mind will not be categorized
summarized listed bar-coded
outlined tee-shirted labeled
uniformed symmetried
homogenized only added to.
Beauty not standards You cannot
standardize what is beautiful
The standards are beauty
of the earth unless you bust it apart
its wildness its wild beauty gone—
standard. Poetry is mind trance
transition to what is beautiful
no desire no wanting free-thinking
earth poems are love poems
are earth poems are love poems
are earth poems in the music and
song and beat of it swinging
jazz mind that knocks you out
with the fact of beautiful soul.

Dan Sklar

Selecting Tunes For the Roadtrip

The trick is to anticipate yourself
a thousand miles from now
on a gravel road in North Dakota
or under wide Montana skies
where all you'll want
is to enhance the mood.
For this, choose older blues,
acoustic bass to suit the two lanes,
Asian Flute and Native drumming,
folk tunes and rare oldies
that tell tales
familiar, like old friends
who lead you
back to yourself, to that place
you strive for, that place
you live for, that place
where the music in you
is all you need.

Charles Rossiter

Rock and Roll Shamans

The first time I noted the mechanics of it
I was almost 35.
Mick Jagger was doing it
at Foxboro Stadium.
Raising energy.
Commanding Energy.
Drumming it out of the wood
and steel
beneath his pounding feet,
And sending it out to us
through his outstretched hand;
through the bodies
of the crowd.

I'd felt it before then,
of course.
The Beatles stomped their feet,
tapped them, actually,
and I was one of the millions
who felt it.
And there was Ray Charles
and Jim Morrison
and others I can't recall.
I didn't have a name for
what they were raising
in me.
Nervous parents called it sex.

Rock and roll
sex
energy
magic
I've felt them all.
And today,
watching the Fabulous Thunderbirds perform
in South Station,
amid trains arriving & commuters departing,

a lead singer bewitched me again
as I stood in the back row.

I wonder about these rock & roll guys
and groupie girls.
Do they know what they're invoking,
and responding to?
Do they recognize the ancient heartbeat of the Earth Mother?
The throbbing drive of the Primal Father?
They who answer
whenever a foot comes down hard,
and then comes down again,
and again,
and then again.

By whatever name...
It's in the ground.
It's in the blood.
It's in the music.
Our parents were right to be afraid.
Like the superstitious natives
they'd seen on TV,
they were running from an erupting
volcano.

Beverly Tricco

Basic Theology

—If you want I can lay it all out
   like a pack of cards with a snap
   of pasteboard and no wonders.
—Go right ahead.

—God is the shape of a surprised mouth
   after the kiss, before the wound.
   God is the tension that lovers breathe
   in you and in me and I am afraid
   that you are suffocating.
—No. Begin again.

—God is the blood left on the thorn
   the blood coloring the rose,
   the sun as it sinks. It rises
   up your back, your neck and
   is real, more real than—
—No. Begin again. Speak clearly.

—God is not real unless space
   is made and space must be made
   between your books and the newspaper,
   between paychecks and coffee breaks.
   And you should know that no church is serious
   and all the temples are bad jokes.
   You should know that none of this
   is very important—

—No—
—But listen! Listen as I scrape
   laughter from my lungs. Listen,
   I am praying in pain the only
   prayer I know. I am praying
   to God clothed in your eyes,
   your body. Don't ask
   what I'm laughing at. I want you
   to leap and know that you will fall,
   that the cards won't catch you.

Do you think my dry throat is
is an accident?

—What are your sources?
—A silent heron, watching.
The low pull of the tides,
a ribbon of highway up and down
this coast. The curve of your thighs,
the root of my tongue. I want you
to leap, because the leap is joyous
and the fall will only break you
and my sources don't matter.

Mark J. Mitchell

Building a Compost Pile

is not unlike building a poem: making something
out of nothing, turning straw into gold, garbage into loam.
Taking what others would throw out:
eggshells, apple peels, coffee grounds,
newspapers full of cumbersome verbiage,
banana skins, grapefruit rinds, grass clippings,
and adding to it daily.

If it seems like nothing's happening, you're wrong.
In the dark, heat and pressure build;
things begin to break down and add up.
Turn, aerate, let it breathe. Add water.
Add worms. Add eye of newt, and bacteria.

It's earthy as a river; it smells like a stable floor.
Are those critics I hear, typing away,
or crickets in the corner of the woodpile?
How do you know when it's done?
Well, you don't, you just abandon it,
to misquote Paul Verlaine. But when you scoop
some out, it's moist and dark as chocolate torte,
black gold; this compost, this humus, it's a richness
you can never get enough of.

Barbara Crooker

We Are the Trees

Deep into the glen we pull you.

Our red-brown trunks
have heartlines
          tiredlines
          lifelines

Come here
Sleep under us

Don't go to the wide open field
Come to the pine forest
the oak at the river's edge

Lie on the pine needle floor
look straight up
far as you can
We seem to converge
never do

Don't be afraid
of the cold mountain lake

Hug one of us first
You won't drown

Don't be afraid
to hitch home on the road

Rub your palms up and down us
We feel it everywhere

With the full moon between us
in the chilly dawn
At twilight
when the last bird song stops

our current flows
from leaves to roots to you

We are the trees
We are old
We know so much

S. Allyx Kronenberg

Becoming the Moon

Dream of things old and foreign.
A medieval castle. An Eskimo drum.
Clasp the trees. Dance circles. Read a poem.

The moon knows a thousand poems. She reads
them sleeping. Every one is quiet yet equally wild.

Say nothing to the factories, the rivers,
the sick swan. Cast your light, indiscriminate
and cool, on the great machines that sit,
so very still, so innocent, so mortal, in the night.

There is nothing for you but to shine.

Anne Coray

Architect

For Eugene Sternberg

Think the man on the other side
of the deli composing a perfect egg
salad on rye with the darkest green
garnish, an eden-delight my tongue
weeps for, or Sophie refusing to fold
carelessly at the Speed-o-Mat
shaping perfect shirts on wire skeletons
and trousers seam to seam, think
Carmen cleaning rooms at the Blue Dove
Inn against her will   still
she draws the night shades meticulously
arranges mints on impeccable pillows,

and you with your fine disregard for all but
nature's random invitation to fill space with
this and that and the ten thousand things
            an architect's sketch: love
            's holy madness defying
            the raw law of gravity.
(*Ya' gotta' ask what it means*, the jazz
man says, *ya' ain't never gonna' know*)

beauty utters itself
no need to speak it.

Rita Brady Kiefer

Sometimes She Is You

Why is heaven always up there,
In the shining stars

Sometimes the One is not
A shower of stars

Sometimes she does not shine,
But falls like snow
And you fall with her
Not knowing, only trusting
You'll land or you'll be carried with the wind

Sometimes she's an autumn leaf,
Falling to the ground and crumbling
And you wait patiently for something new to grow

Sometimes she's a pebble you've
Tossed in a murky pond
Swirls of circles grow until
They fade away

Sometimes she is the wind
Rustling through trees,
Carrying the coyotes' howl through the night
And you trust that if
You weren't there to hear it,
She'd go on carrying it anyway

Sometimes she's a soft mist
In the foggy dark
Your eyes play tricks on you
Or maybe your soul is seeing for once,
One lone woman, digging in the sand,
In the dark.

Carey Raven Star Robin

Drive-By

Sparrow,
flattened on the tarmac
unnoticed by the rush of shoppers
as you slowly shrivel in the sun
I want to blow tobacco up your beak
I want to wish you a good journey
I want to sing you a prayer
but there are strangers around
and they are not like me
they would not understand
why this crazy Indian woman
was acting so weird in the parking lot
or worse yet,
someone might come over and
try to have a free Native American spiritual experience
and maybe write a book about it
so I pinch a little sage from the bundle on my dashboard,
crumble a little tobacco from the ashtray,
and drive over to you, opening the car door
to lay an offering at your head
then revving my engine to make a quick get away
from spiritual drive-by.

Sara Littlecrow-Russell

Untitled

(1)

I want to go into the woods
deep into the woods
where the moose stands
where she suckles her calf
where the deer bed down
unmolested
where the river runs unchained
and the moss floor spreads
its soft invitation
far from the timekeepers
the gearshifters
the hum of tires
the whir of machines
far from the buzz of business
the camaraderie of coffee shops
away from asphalt and steel
the man-made hives of plenty
the hollows of want
away from trivia and plastic
waste and debris
out to where my sleeve
does not rub
another human sleeve
out to where my arm
is limb of tree
my hand a leaf
my foot—root
out to where nature is nature
unblemished
in all its quiet
in all its healing
in all its lovely insistence
saying: Come
saying: Rest

(2)

If you're looking for me
I have gone
with the scent of honeysuckle
on my skin and in my mind
clouds—the white billowy kind—
drifting gently through with no claim.

Sylvia Merrill Beaupré

Blessed. Again!

When the lights came up I was *bathed*, baby, *bathed* I'm telling you, in the most sickly lime color. It was as if that psychopathic sexual killer I dreamed about last night had *vomited*, I'm telling you, just *vomited* limes all over me.

There I was, darlin', just sitting there, in the middle of the stage. Ain't nothin' else but me there. Except that color, of course, which I felt as a *physical presence*. An *entity*, honey. And I was just about to start wondering if it indeed *was* an entity and if mebbe I'd been taken over, like in those Sci-fi shows, you know, when I started *singing*!

Now this is what they mean when they say *surreal*, honey, 'cos I'm sitting there bathed in this serial killer's vomit, and I'm singing "Spiritu Sanctu." And my voice is loud and strong, and I don't know if I'm praising God or saying "Help," but my voice is *filling* that place. What place? I don't know, sweetheart, but I was sure filling it up. Then it changed, you know…I went from that loud sonorous thing to "Es-spiritu-es/es-es-spiritu/es-es-sanctu." You know, like I was in the *groove*, baby.

Whaddya mean was I scared? Scared, honey? I was shit terrified. Now you know I ain't superstitious, but I *know* when God visits me.

Jane Spickett

Approaching the Veil, Scientifically

Eyes like stars sparkle and die
and cycle into new stars, new eyes.

The answer is outside our window.
Astronomers look
for the beginning
and find there is no end.

Down to earth
there are frozen lines,
winter trees,
stalled cars in dirty snow,
sorrow over endings.

The real world is through the window,
infinite, ageless.
Though a clear veil
keeps us distant,
the soul of what
we can never prove
keeps us close.

Belinda Subraman

Light Switch

The power goes
and the whole house
shuts off, like a big animal felled
with sudden mercy, flicked
into a sprawling, dark-limbed silence.

I know where the candles are,
but still have to fumble for the matches,
stumble room to room to place them,
these dim wimpy beacons
that leave knee-deep darkness,
shudders of shadow in the corners,
on the stairs.

I put the biggest pillar
in a mayonnaise jar, make a
coat-hanger handle and go about
my business. When I catch my reflection
in a blacked-out window
my own self like a twin car
on a turnpike overpass, I think, Yeah,
this is how I should always do it.
No more groping
for the switch, gambling
that chance will light
the rooms I move through
No, it's B.Y.O.B. from here on out—
Bring Your Own Bulb, carry
your own Light.

Annie Farnsworth

What We Cannot Touch

suffuses life, plays us like a cello.
Moves us to move beyond
our convenient huts of knowledge
drives us into our unknown
uninhabited wilds.
On the banks of the river
that flows within each
mind sits. Avoids the stream.
Fashions from mud, twigs and leaves
containers for what we seek
and hands them back as metaphor—
the ritual's intricate chalice
empty of drink.
The Hindu father
dips his finger into honey
and on the tongue of his child
traces *Om*. The Navajo mother
touches corn pollen
to her infant's eyes
where a priest would sprinkle water
or a rabbi pour into a newborn's mouth
his thimbleful of wine.
Alchemists seek the philosopher's stone.
Others, the water of life.
But no traveler has ever found it.
No map can deliver us to its shore.
Although we have carried it
from body to body
perhaps sought it in silence
perhaps felt it flood the tenth gate
between our eyes
where unperceived it glistens
come inside.

Kathryn Kruger

Fly-Fishing For Sharks

Others count, but she sees
numbers and letters in gaudy patterns,
spends her days staring at the sea,
her nights in the arms of a spiral galaxy
then savors the moment of waking and not knowing
who or where she is.
She wants to shed lines of the past,
feel scraped clean.
Sometimes safety is unbearable, she reminds
herself as she sees *Fly-Fishing For Sharks*
on the lower shelf
or a 7-inch barbed lure on the top shelf of
PawPaw's beach house,
promise left from a life no longer lived.
Her fortune cookie said not *A windfall*,
but: *There is time enough to take
a different path*; so she's fishing among
pools of letters and numbers,
trying to string them
into a daring message for tomorrow.

Susan Terris

Afterword

This book is a prime example of why poetry is non-fiction. The poems in *Hunger Enough* are not about trivialities, but about the matter of life—both the stuff we consume that may make us complicit with oppression in third world countries and the adjustments we may make in our lives in an attempt to limit our complicity.

In *Hunger Enough*, as in the lecture series *Living Spiritually in a Consumer Society*, from which the idea for this book arose, the objective has never been to create guilt but to observe with honesty our economic connections to social injustice and ecological deterioration. The lectures provided information on local efforts as much as they explored the larger connections. One of the sessions at the Wooster Church, which is a good example of this, was about how working to stop pollution of a local watershed beginning at its source is the way to start addressing the dead zone the size of New Jersey at the mouth of the Mississippi.

Guilt, except perhaps in intensely personal situations, is not a particularly effective motivator. When a two-income family, for convenience sake, eats dinner at a fast-food restaurant, which obtains its fries from soil deadened to all flora except its brand of spud, instead of preparing a dinner from organically grown food purchased at the local farmers market, that family doesn't need an ethical lecture.

Everyone is differently adapted to the consumer society, and I am convinced that most people have a natural desire to do what they perceive is correct. In our relation to our consumption, we often least live up to our beliefs, because most of us know little about the connections between the stuff we consume and the rest of the world.

Perfection, especially in relationship to our consumption, is an existential impossibility. The positive desire to do the right thing, if it becomes obsessive, can freeze a person in inaction. For the most part, there are only more or less positive consumer decisions. To consume is in some ways to be imperfect. And consume we must. Your editor, Nita Penfold, has struck the appropriate stance in making selections for this book. I hope you have read her Introduction. I am convinced that at least in the United States where we are caught up in our things, the people who will bring us to ourselves and our deepest interconnections are not people seeking perfection but uncomfortable people struggling for simple understandings, people who are seeking to move from questioning why the items we buy have not made us happy, to understanding that consumption choices are available or can be made available, which not only enhance our lives but enhance the interconnected web of all existence.

By choosing to focus on our weaknesses and our hopes, Nita has made selections that reach the deeper truths of our everyday economic transactions. These choices are also the stuff from which the best poetry arises, the non-fiction foundation for statistical truth.

—Rev. Jim Bosveld
November 1, 2003

Contributor Notes

Tim Amsden, Rama NM, worked for the U.S. Environmental Protection Agency for 25 years and now lives in the wilds of New Mexico. His work has been published in *Potpourri, Poetry Motel, Out of Line*, and in the anthology, *A Kiss is Still a Kiss* from Tallgrass Writers' Guild. **The Abundant Cow**

Jan Lee Ande, Portland OR. Books include *Instructions for Walking on Water* (Ashland Poetry Press, 2001) and *Reliquary* (Texas Review Press, 2003). Her poems appear in *New Letters, Image* and others. She teaches poetry, poetics, and history of religions at Union Institute and University. **The Naming Of Things**

Antler, Milwaukee WI. Poet Laureate of Milwaukee, Antler is author of *Selected Poems* (Soft Skull Press, NYC, 2000). His work appears in *An Eye For an Eye Makes the Whole World Blind*, and *Poets Against the War*. **Star-Struck Utopias of the 21ˢᵗ Century, Hearing the Echo**

Miriam Axel-Lute, Albany NY. Poetry has appeared in many journals and in the anthology, *Touched by Eros*. She was a finalist in the 2000 Allen Ginsberg Awards. Her chapbook, *Souls Like Mockingbirds*, is available at www.mjoy.org. **Souls Like Mockingbirds**

Edward Beatty, Franklin Grove IL. Beatty's work has appeared in or is forthcoming in *Nimrod, Willow Review, Sunstone, The Bitter Oleander, Potpourri, Parting Gifts, Flyway*, and *Mid-America Poetry Review*. **Development, Career**

Sylvia Merrill Beaupré, Weare NH. Beaupré finds inspiration and peace in fields and woods near her childhood home of Weare NH. Small presses and *Yankee* have published her poetry. She is the author of *Common Ground*, a chapbook about a New England village. **Untitled**

Miriam Ben-Yaacov, Omaha NE, teaches in order to learn: yoga to round the harsh edges of life, writing to know what she believes. Her worldview is colored by her parents' Eastern European Jewish heritage, her South African roots, her relationship with Gideon, a Sabra (Israeli born), and their two sons. **Ways to World Peace**

Douglas Blazek, Sacramento CA. Blazek's work has appeared in *American Poetry Review, Chelsea, The Nation, Agni, Ploughshares, Ironwood*, and *TriQuarterly*. His books include: *Exercises in Memorizing Myself, Flux and Reflux*, and *Edible Fire*. **Glut of Privilege**

Rema Boscov, Leverett MA. **Valentine, After September 11; Valentine in Red, Black and Blue**

James L. Bosveld, Columbus OH. Unitarian Universalist minister, Rev. Jim Bosveld conceptualized the lecture series, *Living Spiritually in a Consumer Society*, which was first sponsored by the Unitarian Universalist Congregation East (Columbus) and then the Wayne County UU Church in Wooster Ohio. He is an advocate for the poor with a background at Legal Aid Society of Columbus where he developed expertise in housing and consumer issues. Jim is also CFO of Pudding House Publications and is frequently found staffing Pudding House and UU Poets' exhibits. He is currently writing a book on 14 pro-active UU characters who helped shape thinking over the generations. **Afterword.**

Jennifer Bosveld, Columbus OH. Jen's poems appear in *Heaven Bone, Chiron Review, The Sun, Wind*, and hundreds of other journals. She is text author and editor of *Elastic Ekphrastic: Poems on Art / Poets on Tour* (2003), editor of *Prayers to Protest: Poems that Center & Bless Us* (1998) and several other anthologies, and author of *The Magic Fish:*

Poems on an Edward Boccia Sketchbook (2002). Her work appears in James Percoco's *Divided We Stand: Teaching about Conflict in U.S. History* (Heinemann, 2001), the college textbook *Discovering Communities: The Reading/Writing Connection* (McGraw Hill, 1997), and *Coffeehouse Poetry* (Bottom Dog Press, 1996). She emcees the annual Clearwater Coffeehouse at the UUA General Assembly. Jennifer received The Pioneer Award from the National Association for Poetry Therapy, a Columbus *Dispatch* Community Service Award, and an Ohio Arts Council Individual Artist Fellowship. **Foreword, Real Abundance.**

Richard Alan Bunch, Davis CA. Bunch's work includes *Summer Hawk, A Foggy Morning*, and *Sacred Space*. His poems have appeared in *Haight Ashbury Literary Journal, Poetry New Zealand, Oregon Review,* and the *Windsor Review*. **Voyages**

Ann Cefola, Scarsdale NY. Cefola's poetry (www.anncefola.com) has been published in *California Quarterly, Confrontation*, and *The Louisville Review*. She won the 2001 Robert Penn Warren Award judged by John Ashbery and has an MFA in poetry from Sarah Lawrence College. **Price Club**

SuzAnne C. Cole, Houston TX, a former English instructor, wrote *To Our Heart's Content: Meditations for Women Turning 50*. She's published essays, poetry, plays, and short fiction in a wide range of commercial and literary publications. She tries to avoid materialism. **Confinement**

Peter Cooley, Jefferson LA, received his Ph.D. from the University of Iowa and is currently teaching creative writing at Tulane University in New Orleans. He has published 7 books of poetry. His newest volume, *A Place Made of Starlight*, was released in 2003. **Incantation**

Anne Coray, Port Alsworth AK, lives at her birthplace on remote Qizhjeh Vena (Lake Clark) in Southwestern Alaska. Her poetry has appeared in *Green Mountains Review, RATTLE, The Women's Review of Books*, and elsewhere. Her chapbook *Ivory* was published by Anabiosis Press. **Directions, Becoming the Moon**

Stephen Corey, Athens GA. Corey's 10th poetry collection, *There Is No Finished World*, was published by White Pine Press in the fall of 2003. His poems, essays, and reviews have appeared in numerous journals and anthologies in the past 25 years, and he is associate editor of *The Georgia Review*. **The Tempest**

Barbara Crooker, Fogelsville PA, recently won the Thomas Merton Poetry of the Sacred Award (Stanley Kunitz, judge), the "April is the Cruelest Month" award from Poets and Writers, and was a finalist for the Foley Poetry Award from *America*. She received three Fellowships in Literature from the Pennsylvania Council on the Arts. **Barbie and Ken Maximize Their Options, From the Museum of Natural History, Building a Compost Pile**

Daniel Dancer, Mosier OR, is the founder of Rowena Wilds, a 200-acre, model environmental development near Hood River where he lives in his home built of recycled and Earth-friendly materials. An environmental artist, Dancer has a master's degree in psychology from the University of Kansas. **Breaking the Spell, cover photographer**

Roger Davies, Nova Scotia, Canada, puts his experience into poems when the words come to him and shares them in e-mails with friends and family. Now a grandfather, he lives by the sea in Nova Scotia. **Melting Into the World**

Mary Krane Derr, Chicago IL, has published poetry in various magazines including *Many Mountains Moving, Sacred Journey*, and *Pudding Magazine, the International Journal of Applied Poetry*. Her environmental activism is linked to her personal experience of two pollution-related diseases, asthma and endometriosis. **Why Should I Care**

Richard Downing, Hudson FL, has published *The Waking Rooms*, a novel, and poetry and short stories in various journals including *Crosscurrents* and *Potomac Review*. He won New Delta Review's 2003 Matt Clark Prize for Poetry and founded the environmental group, Save Our Naturecoast. **Palm Lines**

Max Roland Ekstrom, Watertown MA, lives and works in the Boston area. His first chapbook is *Maiden Voyage*. **Career Guy Poem**

Karen Ethelsdattar, Union City NJ, is a poet and liturgist whose work has appeared in *Womanspirit, Off Our Backs, Calyx, Mothering,* Starhawk's book *The Spiral Dance*. Her book *Earthwalking and other poems* was published in 2002 by Xlibris, and her second book, *Thou Art a Woman & Other Poems*, was published in 2003 by Xlibris. **Making Play**

Annie Farnsworth, Arundel ME, is the editor/publisher of *Animus*. Her work has appeared or is forthcoming in *RATTLE, The Café Review, Puckerbrush Review, The Aurorean*, and *Off the Coast*. She is the 2003 recipient of *Words & Images Magazine*'s Stephen Dunn Poetry Award, and the 2003 winner of *Dark Moon Lilith*'s poetry competition. **What I Thought Of At WalMart, Light Switch**

David Feela, Cortez CO, writes and teaches writing. He publishes a monthly column for *Inside/Outside Magazine*, which appears in the Four Corners region. See www.geocities.com/feelasophy. **Surreal Estate**

Maureen Tolman Flannery, Evanston IL, was raised in a Wyoming ranch family & now lives in Chicago. She is an award-winning poet and the author of *Secret of the Rising Up: Poems of Mexico* and *Remembered into Life*. **Collector, Absence of Benign Deprivation**

John Grey, Providence RI, is an Australian-born poet, playwright, musician. His work appears in *South Carolina Review, Bogg, GSU Review, Texas Poetry Calendar*, and *Blueline*. **Devolution**

Karen Howland, Sheboygan WI, is an internationally published poet, professional moodler, holistic nurse, and award-winning singer. She teaches writing circles across the Midwest and swims with dolphins when she can. **Factory Ecstasy**

Daniel Hunter, Medina OH, is an insurance agent by day and poet by night. Dan holds a B.A. in English from The College of Wooster and is a past first prize winner for poetry at the Midwest Writers' Conference. **Call to Communion**

Mary Junge, Eden Prairie MN. Minneapolis poet and social activist Mary Junge recently published *Express Train*, a chapbook (Pudding House Publications, 2002). Her poetry has been published in a variety of journals, including the 2002 issue of *Water~Stone*. **In Consideration of Things**

Elizabeth Kerlikowske, Kalamazoo MI, teaches at Kellogg Community College in Battle Creek, the town that always smells like morning. She is the author of three chapbooks of poetry and has twice won the Detroit Auto Dealer's Short Story contest. Mother of three, she writes in a tree house to get away from it all. **Shelling Peas**

Charles Kesler, Dallas TX, has been published in *Pudding, WebWUURKS, Pearl, Chiron Review, The Aurorean,* and many other small press publications. **What's Next?**

Rita Brady Kiefer, Evergreen CO. **Architect**

Joan Payne Kincaid, Sea Cliff NY. Nominated for Pushcart Prizes in 1998 and 1999, Joan Payne Kincaid publishes in journals and anthologies in the US and abroad; her three new CDs, with music and accompaniment by Dick Metcalf, are available. **Twilight Sleep**

David Kowalczyk, Kenmore NY. Kowalczyk's fiction and poetry have appeared in a host of literary journals and anthologies, including *California Quarterly, Maryland Review*, and

Pure Light. He was awarded the Just Buffalo Literary Center's 2001 Poetry Fellowship. **Logic of Conspicuous Consumption**

S. Allyx Kronenberg, Santa Monica CA, has two poetry books published: *Always, I Was Getting Ready To Go* (Black Heron Press) and *Incantations of the Grinning Dream Woman* (Sagittarius Press), and has poetry in *The California Quarterly, The Manhattan Poetry Review,* and *Poetry Now,* among others. **We Are the Trees**

Kathryn Kruger, Warrenville IL. Kruger's first collection of poetry, *Solstice*, won the 2001 chapbook contest for Poetic Matrix, and her poem "Fallen" was nominated for a Pushcart Prize. Her work has appeared in *Water-Stone Magazine, Heart, Tar River Poetry, Sacred Journey,* and *Sufi Magazine.* **What We Cannot Touch**

Mary Laufer, Forest Grove OR. Laufer's work appears in *Learning to Glow, a Nuclear Reader* (University of Arizona Press, 2000) and *Proposing on the Brooklyn Bridge* (Grayson Books, 2003), as well as nationally in journals and newspapers. **At The Top of the Food Chain, Our Conscience**

Gabrielle LeMay, New York NY, has been devoted to poetry for more than 20 years and has won awards from *The Writer's Voice*, The Academy of American Poets, and Hunter College, where she received her MFA in 2001. Her work has appeared in *Blue Mesa Review, The Ledge, Poems & Plays,* and *Rattapallax.* **Nativity**

Ellen Lindquist, Atlanta GA, is a Pushcart Prize-nominated writer with work in *The Small Pond Magazine, 5 a.m.*, and *US 1 Worksheets.* Her story "Cuppa" was a winner of *Fiction Inferno*'s Very Short Fiction contest. **How the Pitiless Sprinkler Ushered in the Apocalypse**

Lou Lipsitz, Chapel Hill NC, is a psychotherapist and poet who has published three books of poems and his work has been included in numerous anthologies. His most recent book is *Seeking The Hook* (Signal Books, 1997). www.loulipsitz.com. **Watching the TV Version Of The Holocaust**

Sara Littlecrow-Russell, Hyde Park MA, is Anishinaabe-Han Metis, an activist, and Public Interest Law Fellow at Northeastern School of Law in Boston. Her poetry has appeared in the anthologies *Sister Nations: Native American Women Writing On Community, Touched by Eros, All Our Relations: Native Struggles for Land and Life*, and a variety of other journals. **I Become A Political Traitor, Drive-By**

Lisa Martinović, Sebastopol CA, is an artist, essayist, and slam poet. She is marketing her new screenplay, a scorching political satire. www.slaminatrix.com. **Is That Chicken Organic?**

James McGrath, Santa Fe NM, is a poet, artist, and teacher and creator of the narrative poetry for the PBS *American Indian Artist Series*. His work has been published in *MAN! Magazine, Dakotah Territory, Arizona Highways* and in Sarasota Press' *Animals in Poetry Anthology.* **Speaking With Magpies**

Robert Aquinas McNally, Concord CA, has published three poetry chapbooks, and he is the author or co-author of eight nonfiction books, with the ninth in progress. **Their Gathering**

María Meléndez, Davis CA, has published poetry and short stories in a variety of journals, including *Puerto del Sol* and *Ecological Restoration.* Her first chapbook of poetry, *Base Pairs*, was published in 2001 by Swan Scythe Press (www.swanscythe.com). **Collections of Nearly Unlovable Spaces**

Mark J. Mitchell, San Francisco CA, studied writing at UC Santa Cruz under Raymond Carver, George Hitchcock, and Barbara Hull. His work has appeared in *kayak, Blue*

Unicorn, Bogg, and *Santa Barbara Review* among many others. He lives in San Francisco with his wife, the filmmaker Joan Juster. **Basic Theology**

Jacqueline Moore, Portland ME, is retired, dividing the year between the city and the backwoods. Her poems have appeared in *Off Our Backs, The New Jersey Poetry Journal, Green Mountains Review, Maine Times, The Beloit Poetry Journal, Visions International,* and *The Dissident.* **Dominion**

Gwendolyn Morgan, Portland OR. A native Oregonian, Morgan holds a MFA in Creative Writing from Goddard College and a M.Div. from San Francisco Theological Seminary. Her poetry has been published in *The Dakotah, Kalliope, Kinesis* and *Mudfish,* among other places. Gwendolyn was recently awarded writing residencies at Caldera and Soapstone for *White Clay, Red Ocher,* her poetry manuscript. **Desire**

Tim Myers, Santa Clara CA, is a writer, songwriter, and professional storyteller teaching at Santa Clara University. His children's book *Basho and the Fox* was read on NPR and made the New York *Times* bestseller list; he also won a national poetry contest judged by John Updike. **Toys**

Sheryl L. Nelms, Azle TX, has had 8 collections of poetry published; her most recent collection, *Tap Dancing On My Brain,* is due out from Kitty Litter Press. She makes her living as an insurance adjuster and is also a painter, weaver and dirt biker. **Feng Shui**

Julia Older, Hancock NH. Older's collections include *The Ossabaw Book of Hours* and *City In the Sky* (Oyster River Press, 2001) and *Hermaphroditus in America* (Appledore Books, 2000). Her poetry and prose have been published in *The New Yorker, New Directions, Nimrod International,* and elsewhere. **Valiant Soldiers**

Lee Patton, Denver CO, writes poetry, fiction, and drama. His poetry has appeared in *The Threepenny Review, The Massachusetts Review, The California Quarterly,* and *Hawaii-Pacific Review.* **Dismantling Hell at the Old Dump**

Nita Penfold, Melrose MA, received her master's in Writing from Lesley University and her Doctorate in Divinity from Matthew Fox's University of Creation Spirituality in Oakland CA. Her poetry has been published widely, including two chapbooks from Pudding House Publications. **Discipline**

Tamra Plotnick, Brooklyn NY. Plotnick's writing has appeared in various publications, including *Global City Review* and *A Gathering of Tribes #8.* She has recently completed a novel. **This Just In...**

Carey Raven Star Robin, Warrenville IL, is a writer and teacher. After a four-day vision quest, she was gifted with her true name. Currently, she is working on a novel about modern marriages. **Sometimes She Is You**

Charles Rossiter, Oak Park IL, is an NEA Fellowship recipient, Pushcart nominee, and host of the international audio website, poetrypoetry.com. He's much published in literary magazines and anthologies, and his work has been featured in NPR and numerous state-wide public radio networks. **Selecting Tunes For the Roadtrip**

Aubrey Ryan, Davenport IA, is a theatre major at Millikin University and has been published in *The Wabash Review* and *Collage Literary Journal.* She was the 2002 winner of the Collage Award for Outstanding Poetry. **My Cellmate the Bear**

Dennis Saleh, Seaside CA. Saleh's poetry, prose, and artwork appear widely in magazines and journals such as *Psychological Perspectives* and *ArtLife.* His poems are in two recent California anthologies, *How Much Earth* and *The Geography of Home.* **The Eagle**

Nicholas Samaras, Palm Harbor FL. Samaras' first book, *Hands of the Saddlemaker,* won the Yale Series of Younger Poets Award. He has just completed a new manuscript of poetry which is looking for a publisher. Currently, he teaches at the University of South Florida and directs the Writers Voice Program in Tampa. **The History of the Twenty-First Century**

Shoshauna Shy, Madison WI. Shy's poems have been included in anthologies produced by Pudding House Publications, Wild Dove Studio & Press, Grayson Books, and Random House. Her chapbook, *Souped-Up on the Must-Drive Syndrome* was published by Pudding House in 2000. **The Suggestion of Slivers**

Dan Sklar, South Hamilton MA, teaches writing at Endicott College. His recent publications include *Rising, Revolve, bowWow*, and *Steam Ticket*. **Poetry Mind**

Rick Smith, Alta Loma CA, is a clinical psychologist who co-directs Back In the Saddle, a residential program for brain-damaged adults in Apple Valley CA. He plays harmonica for the Hangan Brothers (recent release, *Mars Market*) and his latest book is *The Wren Notebook* (Lummox Press, 2000). **Found in Dave's Things**

S. Soil, Thornhill ON Canada. Sophie Soil is an artist/craftsperson who won 1st & 2nd prizes at the Canadian Exhibition. She has published poetry/prose in various magazines and anthologies. **Sellout**

Jane Spickett, Arlington, MA, is a photographer, writer, and ceremonialist—a pilgrim-artist. As a recovering English person, she feels that de-Anglicizing reveals that mind, heart and soul are capable of infinite expansion. **Blessed. Again!**

Dalene Stull, Danville OH, lives on a 30-acre farm where she writes and teaches piano. Her poems have appeared in *Kansas Quarterly, The Heartlands Today, The Listening Eye, The Cincinnati Poetry Review*, and other journals, as well as state award books. **Seeds**

Belinda Subraman, El Paso TX, has published many books through Vergin Press, including *Voces Frontierizas, The Gulf War: Many Perspectives, Earth Tones, Images of Jim Morrison*, and *Henry Miller and My Big Sur Days*. She balances her life as a writer and RN by painting, sculpting, and political activism. **Approaching the Veil, Scientifically**

Susan Terris, San Francisco CA. Terris' book *Fire Is Favorable To The Dreamer* has just been published by Arctos Press. In 2004, Adastra Press will publish her chapbook *Poetic License*, and Marsh Hawk Press will publish her third full-length book, *Natural Defenses*. **What Has Been Lost, Fly-Fishing For Sharks**

Beverly Tricco, Randolph MA, sees herself as a Jack of all arts and Master of none. Her most consistent fascinations are her children, the relationship between the magic and the mundane, and what it means to be a human being. **Rock and Roll Shamans**

Helen Tzagoloff, New York NY, has poems in *New York Quarterly, The MacGuffin, Blueline, Riverrun, Nightsun* and others. She was the First Place Winner in the Icarus International 2002 literary competition and a chapbook, *Waiting*, was published in the New School Poetry Chapbook series. **Government at Work**

Ellen Waterston, Bend OR. Waterston's poetry has appeared in *West Wind Review, Range* magazine, and *Woven In The Wind*, published by Houghton Mifflin. Her non-fiction memoir *Then There Was No Mountain* (Roberts Rinehart Publishers) was released October of 2003. **Hollow Hearts**

Ellen Wehle, Winthrop MA, quit a job in advertising in order to write full time. She is currently the poetry editor at *Agni*. *Acedia*

Debra McCorkle Wells, Statesboro GA, owns a shop in the mountains of North Carolina. She writes essays and poetry in the minutes between mothering and rearranging her (largely secondhand) inventory. **if it ain't been in a pawn shop**

Arisa White, Brooklyn NY, graduated from Sarah Lawrence College with a major in creative writing and literature. Her work has appeared in *African Voices, A Gathering of Tribes*, and *Sarah Lawrence Magazine*. She currently lives in Queens NY and works for a nonprofit. **RiteAid**

David E. Williams, Gloucester MA, is a human service worker living in Massachusetts. His work has been published in *Three Mile River, Black Hat Press,* and *Poetry Motel.* **The Silver Lining, On the Planet Logo**

Janna Willoughby, Buffalo NY, is a poet, artist, and musician from Buffalo, NY, 21 years old, currently enrolled as a senior at Warren Wilson College in Asheville, NC. She is majoring in Integrative Studies: Entrepreneurial Arts in order to open her own website to sell varied forms of art. **Dreams Make Wishes In My Existence Of Thrift**